Numerology
for
Healing

Your Personal Numbers as the Key to a Healthier Life

MICHAEL BRILL

Destiny Books

Rochester, Vermont

Destiny Books
One Park Street
Rochester, Vermont 05767
www.DestinyBooks.com

Destiny Books is a division of Inner Traditions International

Library of Congress Cataloging-in-Publication Data

Brill, Michael (Michael Richard)
  Numerology for healing : your personal numbers as the key to a healthier life / Michael Brill.
     p. cm.
  Includes bibliographical references.
  Summary: "A unique approach to using numerology to identify life challenges and karmic lessons to heal emotional and physical problems"—Provided by publisher.
  ISBN 978-1-59477-236-8 (pbk.)
  1. Numerology. 2. Healing—Miscellanea. 3. Health—Miscellanea. I. Title.
  BF1623.P9B66 2009
  133.3'35—dc22

                                                                                    2008041793

Printed and bound in the United States by Lake Book Manufacturing

10 9 8 7 6 5 4 3 2 1

Text design and layout by Priscilla Baker
This book was typeset in Garamond Premier Pro with Perpetua used as a display typeface.

For more information on the author of this book, including contact information, please visit his website at **www.awakener.com**

Contents

Acknowledgments

GOD, I thank you for your assistance, support, and guidance.

I'd like to thank my mom and dad, Toby, and Curtis for their assistance from the other side.

Thanks to all of my spiritual trainers for helping me to develop the courage to do what I love, not to be loved or to maintain control.

Special thanks to Aleya, Anne, Corinne, Deborah, Devra, Elaine, Joy, Patricia, and Sandy for their friendship, their counsel, and their presence in my life.

There is one more person I would like to thank: my editor at Destiny Books, Jamaica Burns. Jamaica, thank you for your insightful editing; you're the best!

Introduction

Numbers are my passion. Since 1985, I have been developing and practicing a system that melds the sciences of numerology and quantum physics with the concepts of gematria and reincarnation. This system—Cosmic Numerology—is the study of patterns associated with the numbers and letters that make up our potential realities. It can reveal what you have chosen to experience in this life—your challenges, including physical and emotional problems, and their *soulutions* (soul-chosen solutions)—and help you clarify your purpose.

Generally, most people will agree that illness, disease, and physical injury can be caused by stress—rushing around, doing too much, doing too little, genes, exhaustion, impulsiveness, or just bad luck. My belief is that most of our health issues are the result of behavior patterns associated with anxiety and stress, generated by unresolved issues of abandonment and fears of being alone. This anxiety is universal and begins with the illusion of being separated from the energy of the cosmic Source and, then, being physically separated from the "mother source" when the umbilical cord is severed at birth. These core abandonment issues cause us to behave in such a way that we will garner love, recognition, appreciation, and gratitude for what we do and who we are. Or they can lead us to try to control and micromanage every aspect of our lives so that nothing goes wrong and we don't get blamed or humiliated. Both behavior patterns are physically, emotionally, and mentally exhausting—and are the catalysts for our illnesses, diseases, and physical injuries.

Numbers and letters represent the codes of creation, which are generated by cosmic choice. Cosmic Numerology allows us to understand, measure, and interpret combinations of energies as they interact with our realities. It allows us to see the patterns of creation as well as the patterns of our lives. The numeric patterns described in this book correspond to patterns of behavior that are the catalysts for specific illnesses and diseases. The behavior patterns are generated at the soul level prior to incarnating and are influenced and directed by particles and waves of positive and negative energy generated by intention. It is my belief that a soul consciously selects the letters of its name and the numbers for its birthday, along with a specific birth or adoptive family to initiate its life movie. Specific challenges and soulutions are also chosen. The soul comes in, knowing what is ahead and that it has enough grace to successfully accomplish what it came to do in this lifetime.

It is my hope that you will enjoy this book and learn how and why *you* have created the specific challenges and joys in your life. Specifically, this book will help you better understand how and why your behavior patterns helped manifest your health challenges. I also hope to provide you with some soulutions and answers that will assist you on your healing journey.

We will begin by exploring some of the theories behind Cosmic Numerology—the relationship between numbers and the divine energy of creation, reincarnation, and basic human behavior patterns—before moving on to the specifics of how the system works. In chapter 3 you will learn how to identify your own challenge numbers: the achievement number, major and minor life challenges, and karmic lessons. Learning how to interpret these numbers and the personality traits associated with them will help you better understand why you behave the way you do. Chapter 4 will teach you how to identify the soulutions to your challenges and will provide an introduction to numeric daisy chains, a technique that maps the eighty-one basic patterns of human personality and reveals the specific negative behavior patterns associated with each. Identifying and changing just two of the most repetitive patterns can bring profound healing changes to your life. In chapter 5 I detail the numeric qualities of more than two hundred physical and mental conditions and associated symptoms. This section will allow you to explore the direct relationships between your personal numbers—specifically numeric challenges—and the illnesses you have contracted, or created. By revealing your positive and negative tendencies and characteristics, you can learn how to use them to achieve a healthier life. We will conclude with a final look at the choices that lead to illness and those that bring healing.

As you become more familiar with the numbers, it will become increasingly automatic not only to convert letters into their numeric equivalents but also to know the specific qualities associated with each number. The conversion chart for identifying the numeric equivalents of letters appears on page 15 and in miniature at the top of each page. A summary of the positive and negative interpretations of each number appears beginning on page 18. You may find it helpful to flag this page for easy reference as you discover and interpret your numbers.

Approach this book as you would a bountiful meal, to be eaten in small portions and digested slowly. Dessert is revelation and insight. May I show you to your table?

1

The Theories Behind
Cosmic Numerology

As mentioned in the introduction, Cosmic Numerology melds the classical system of numerology; quantum physics, in which absolutes and cause and effect are replaced with potentials and probabilities; the ancient kabbalistic art of gematria, which interprets the energies of letters by converting them to numbers; and the concepts of reincarnation. All of these theories go into analyzing the interrelationships of the energies and events that affect our daily lives and the behavior patterns that are the catalysts for illness.

REINCARNATION AND GOD ENERGY

The concepts of reincarnation are at the core of Cosmic Numerology. Reincarnation revolves around the idea that we consciously choose what we want to experience in each life. Experiences that are not completed within a lifetime will be completed in future lifetimes. Reincarnation is similar to waking up on your birthday and being given a ticket to an amusement park by your parents. You go to the park and, as you enter, you are wowed by all the choices. You spend the whole day at the park riding as many rides as you can. Some you avoid because they are too scary; others you ignore because they are too "babyish" (been there, done that). Some you are not permitted to ride because you don't yet meet the requirements, such as height and age limits, or you need to be accompanied by an adult. At the end of the day you are exhausted from all of the activity. You go home and, just before drifting off to sleep, ask your parents if you can go back tomorrow. They say yes. You drift off to sleep, dreaming of what you intend to do tomorrow.

Each of us is a compilation of GOD energies, which are responsible for all creation. *GOD* stands for Gathering of Deities. Other terms used to describe this energy are Spirit, Source, Cosmos, All That Is, Oneness, Creator, and God. Whatever we call it, this core energy needs to be stepped down to be utilized. We can use a lightning bolt as an analogy. In its pure state, the electricity locked within the lightning can kill us. However, when we harness this power through transformers that can lower its charge, it becomes usable. It can heat our homes, run our factories, cook our food, and light our cities. The same must be done with the GOD energy. In its pure state, it has no form, no intention, no direction: just potential.

The numbers 1–9 represent these deities/energies/base frequencies of creation. Everything in creation can be reduced to a number between 1 and 9. This is how I see the GOD energy transformed. All energy can be seen as frequency waves, composed of combinations of subfrequencies, generated by the blending of the numbers 1–9. There is a transition phase in which these combinations of particles and waves meld to form the energy of creation. This creative energy is the one we are more conscious of—what we may think of as the Big Bang or God. From there, another transition phase leads to the beginning of physicality and development of ego.

We all start as a part of the Whole (i.e., God energy). We then choose to be part of the creative process, to record our experiences in the

Akashic records, by physically extending our soul energy from Source through a transition phase into physicality. Prior to entering this transition phase, we have a conversation with the God energy in which we review our most recent experiences—what the soul has mastered, become proficient at, avoided, or left unfinished. We then create a blueprint of what we intend to experience and contribute in this next incarnation. This blueprint is composed of the letters of our name, the numbers of our birthday, and what family we choose to join. We create this blueprint beforehand, because we know that once we start the transition into physicality, we will lose the memory of who we truly are and what we volunteered to cocreate. It is this temporary "loss of memory" that is the seed of our feelings of abandonment or isolation. As we pass through the transition tube and extend out from Source into physicality, we think to ourselves: What is going on? Where is everybody? Why am I alone? Did I do something wrong? Am I being punished? Why is it dark? Why am I moving? We feel we've been abandoned or "kicked out" with no explanation. Our questions go unanswered and we become anxious, even fearful, thinking we are alone. The process of individuation has begun; we are entering physicality. The EGO (Easing God Out)—our physical body, its emotions and feelings—adopts a behavior pattern of self-protection, a pattern that reinforces the illusion of being apart. We have begun to look outward for validation, rather than inward.

Here is a quick exercise that illustrates this outward-looking mentality: Keep your head in a fixed position and look straight ahead. Now, look up and then look down. Look left and look right. What your eyes see is the extent of your physical reality. As you look outward, everything you see appears to be separate from you. And yet, you and everything you see are parts of the whole that compose this planet. The eyes themselves have no idea that they are connected to anything. They can't "see" the nerves, muscles, blood vessels, and other connections attaching them to the brain.

Unless we look inward to find our connection with the Whole, we will feel incomplete. When we decide to look inward, we must move beyond the initial veils of darkness, where the fears of abandonment and aloneness reside. Once past these veils, the memory of our divinity returns. Our feelings of abandonment end when we remember we didn't *separate* from Source but rather *extended* from Source to become cocreators. We are the eyes of the God energy. We must look inward to see what we have chosen to cocreate.

BASIC HUMAN BEHAVIOR PATTERNS

The innate fear of abandonment or of being alone leads to the creation of four basic behavior patterns. At one end of the behavior spectrum is codependency, a need to have an "other" in your life. On the opposite end of the spectrum is the need for control. Major numbers associated with control are 1, 4, 6, 8, and 9; the major codependency numbers are 1, 2, 6, 7, and 9. As an interesting aside, even numbers usually represent extrovert behaviors, whereas odd numbers represent introvert behaviors.

Codependency can be divided into three subcategories, *clingers, enablers,* and *doers.* Clingers rationalize—"anything is better than being alone"—and, regardless of how they are treated, they find it almost impossible to leave a relationship. Ever disapproved of a loved one's behavior, such as smoking or drinking? Did you still buy that person cigarettes or alcohol? Enablers either assist or allow others to continue self-defeating or addictive behaviors. Doers make themselves indispensable. Their rationale is, "I'll do so much for them, they won't be able to make do without me."

Behavior patterns involving control can be divided into two subgroups. The first consists of individuals who choose not to become emotionally involved or attached to anything. In essence, they hide or deny their emotions and feelings. They reason that if they don't connect to something, they can't be disconnected from it. The most extreme example is the sociopath personality. Individuals in the second controller

	1	2	3	4	5	6	7	8	9
	A	B	C	D	E	F	G	H	I
	J	K	L	M	N	O	P	Q	R
	S	T	U	V	W	X	Y	Z	

8   The Theories Behind Cosmic Numerology

subgroup decide that the safest route is to do for others but not let anyone "do" for them or to them. For example, they will hold the handle of the water fountain so that others may drink with ease but will not let anyone hold the handle for them, fearing that the holder will let go. They feel that "others" cannot be depended upon. (As we will see later, this pattern is one of the catalysts for Alzheimer's disease.)

We all bounce around between the extremes of codependency and control, until we remember our "divineness" and become centered. Our goal is to recognize our issues through our challenges. Once we recognize our patterns, we can alter them to achieve better health and well-being.

The following paragraphs offer some examples of how abandonment anxieties can influence interactions and behaviors at home, within relationships, and at work. I have divided the analysis into personality types I describe as *controllers, clingers, enablers,* and *doers.* Because they rarely listen to their inner Self (for fear of being wrong and, thus, abandoned or humiliated), those who fall into these four patterns are the most susceptible to contracting an illness or disease.

In Family Relationships
- *Controllers* offer money or other materialistic things to "make" someone do what they want him or her to do; or make promises and, then, at the last moment, rescind the agreement or deny ever having made an agreement at all in an effort to exert control over every aspect of that person's life.
- *Clingers* may remain in an unhappy relationship of codependency because they fear an inability to support themselves, or they may leave a relationship but then return due to a lack self-esteem and a fear that no one else would have them.
- *Enablers* repeatedly loan money to or bail out family members who don't accept personal responsibility for their actions.
- *Doers* say, "You can hold the anniversary party here; I'll take care of everything!" Or, "I don't know what you'd do without me!"

In Partnerships

- *Controllers* can be jealous to the point of micromanaging a relationship to prevent being abandoned. They may want to control the relationship because they think they know what is best . . . for everyone.
- *Clingers* say, "How did I get this black eye? I walked into a door," "I can't leave, someday he'll change," or "I can't leave, she needs me!" They often remain in a relationship fearful that no one else would want them.
- *Enablers* make excuses for their partners' lateness, absence, weight, attitude, and so on and in various ways allow or enable the negative behaviors.
- *Doers* shower their beloved with cards, flowers, and gifts to excess, so they'll be loved.

With Friends

- *Controllers* say, "If you don't do this, I'll leave." Or, "If you want me to . . . , then you'll have to . . ."
- *Clingers* say, "Okay, I'll do it, but promise you'll stay." Or, "That's the fifth time you've broken your promise about getting help for your problem."
- *Enablers* may not smoke, but always have matches for those who do. They will give money, or offer support in some other way, to a friend who is an abuser (be it of people, substances, or self).
- *Doers* say, "I'll take care of everything; don't anyone worry!" "I'll wait in line for the tickets. You all can get something to eat."

At Work

- *Controllers* don't delegate, fearful that a task will not be done "correctly." They may also micromanage.
- *Clingers* say, "You want me to work the weekend shift again? This is the sixth consecutive weekend you've asked me to do

this. Okay, just let me call home and cancel my plans, again."

- *Enablers* say, "Don't worry. I'll cover for you," and complete other people's assignments, not out of compassion, but from fear of abandonment.

- *Doers* say, "You need the proposal rewritten by Monday morning and need a hundred copies for distribution? No problem. Do I need help? No, I can do it myself."

CHANGING YOUR NEGATIVE PATTERNS

There is a quick and easy way to determine if abandonment issues are impacting your physical body and your decision-making process. Check the tension level in your body.

Here's a personal example. I had a two o'clock appointment and five hours to drive the two hundred miles to get there. The first hundred miles was over mountain passes where you could safely drive an average speed of about 40 mph, whereas the second hundred miles had an average speed limit of 65–75 mph. Based on this information, there would be plenty of time to get to my appointment, even arriving early. As I crossed the mountains, there was an unusual number of vehicles towing fifth-wheel trailers. Being stuck behind several of these trailers only doing about 10 mph, I began tensing up and worrying about getting to my appointment on time. (My abandonment buttons were being pushed.) Whenever I had the opportunity to pass, I gunned the engine and raced around the vehicle in front of me. I was worried that I would be late and others would think I was unreliable. For the entire trip over the mountains, I passed whatever I could whenever I could. I finally got out of the mountains and onto the flats. As I was coming around a curve, three dump trucks were coming from the opposite direction. The third truck threw a stone, which struck my windshield, chipping the glass and causing a starburst. Had I been coming around that turn ten seconds later, I would not have been hit. It was the universe's way of reminding me to be more patient and trusting and that if I wasn't, there would be consequences.

So, whenever you feel yourself tensing up, becoming impatient, anxious, frustrated, or angry, think about the reason behind your anxiety and acknowledge that abandonment issues are probably at the root. Soulution? Relax, Spirit's in charge.

You can make the choice to change your patterns. Be patient with yourself and remember, anything that's been moving in one direction at great speed cannot easily be stopped and turned around. (Try hitting the reverse switch on a ceiling fan as it runs at high speed and watch how long it takes to reverse itself.)

How do you begin to change a lifelong pattern? You surrender. Finally accepting the fact that you cannot make the universe do your bidding and consciously surrendering to the "All That Is" allows you to begin changing negative patterns. If you still try to force your way, negative particles of energy will continue to accumulate, increasing the probability of exacerbating an existing health condition or of initiating a new one.

Cosmic Numerology can identify the underlying patterns of negative behavior that are the catalysts for an illness or a disease. As a being with free will, you have the option of choosing the direction of your journey. Are you ready to make that choice? Or will you allow yourself to be pulled along by unseen forces fed by fears of abandonment? Do you want to settle for a reactive life or to live a proactive life?

The energy our universe is composed of has both positive and negative electrical charges, with a neutral space between them. Envision a flashlight battery with its positive and negative posts. The protruding post at the top of the battery is the positive energy, which has a quick trip to the exit point. The negative post at the base of the battery uses the same exit point. Because the negative energy has a longer distance to travel, the probability of unexpected encounters with other energies increases. In our lives, these encounters are challenges, which can delay our progress toward our destination. These challenges are activated when we ignore what feels right in our heart, because we lack the courage to follow it. Instead, we'll do things to be loved or to maintain control, fearful of being abandoned or left alone.

There are three major categories of challenges, which we will explore in this book: the achievement number, major and minor life challenges, and karmic lessons. Each of these categories has the potential to attract huge amounts of negatively charged particles of energy, which make them catalysts for illnesses, diseases, and physical injuries.

How do you alter your negative patterns? Begin by learning to honor yourself. Why is this so difficult? Because to do so will likely call down the wrath of those you've always tried to please or control. I call these individuals *spiritual trainers*. Much like hiring a physical trainer to help us get into better physical condition, we enlist spiritual trainers to help us with our spiritual awakening. We audition them; hand them a script; and tell them to question our abilities, our motives, our decisions, and our dreams. We pay them time and a half to work weekends and triple time for holidays and family gatherings.

We write dialogue for them to say to us: "Don't be so selfish." "You've changed." "You're not the person I used to know." "You'll never succeed." "You never do what I want." "You don't care." "That's really stupid." "You think you're better than everyone else." "If you loved me, you would . . ." These are all "hooks" to snag us and draw us back into manipulative relationships, relationships in which we did things to be loved, recognized, appreciated, or thanked, or to maintain control. These are people we wrote into our life scripts to test our resolve and to teach us to honor what we feel (and know) in our hearts to be true. Sometimes this requires us to leave relationships, partnerships, even friendships. Passing these "built-in" tests will allow us to start doing what we love instead of "doing" to be loved or to maintain control.

These trainers will help us remember our divine mission. Remember this in your next interaction with the person who gives you the most grief or aggravates you the most. You may want to give that person a trophy to recognize the quality of his or her performance in following the script you wrote.

It's been my experience that some excellent ways of quickly diminishing the amount of negatively charged particles and opening energetic blockages—whether they're mental, emotional, or physical—are acupuncture, acupressure, use of essential oils, deep tissue massage, and hypnosis. These tools can be effective at dissolving or breaking up energetic blockages. However, if your base patterns don't change, the conditions will return.

The information in this book will help you develop an awareness of your emotional and psychological patterns, allowing you to become proactive in your life choices and improve your health and quality of life. Use of the material presented in this book is not intended to replace the advice of a medical professional. If you have health issues, whether you believe in mainstream or alternative medicine, please seek professional medical advice. To get the most out of the information presented in the following chapters, be totally honest in your assessment of yourself.

2

How Cosmic Numerology Works

Using the letters of your name and the numbers of your birthday, Cosmic Numerology interprets the emotional and psychological characteristics you chose to experience in this lifetime and identifies your personal challenges and their soulutions.

In classical numerology, the letters of a name and the birth numbers represent the patterns and timing of events to be experienced. In Cosmic Numerology, the soul consciously selects these letters and numbers. Focus is placed on the psychological and emotional characteristics that result from combining the letters and numbers of a name. Once the numeric sequence of someone's name and birth data is plotted and the soul-chosen challenges and soulutions are overlaid, a picture of lifelong behavior patterns emerges. These patterns can be the triggers for illnesses, diseases, physical injuries, and the activators of genetic predispositions (e.g., diabetes, heart disease).

The basic concepts outlined in this short chapter are essential for figuring your own challenge numbers (which I walk you through in chapter 3) and understanding the material covered in the rest of the book.

A NOTE ON NAME CHANGES

The name to be used for figuring all of your information is the name that appears on your birth certificate, unless you were adopted or went to court to legally change your name for a reason other than marriage. This is the name chosen by your soul to activate all events for this lifetime.

If you legally changed your name (for reasons other than marriage), the date the court approves the name change becomes your new birthday. You are consciously choosing to start your life over. The date you pick for your name change is vital because it generates a new achievement number and therefore a new set of challenges. What is interesting about a name change is that the new name and birthday will usually have most of the same challenges as the old name and date.

LETTER-TO-NUMBER CONVERSION

The classical conversion chart used to transpose letters into their numeric equivalents is shown below. The letters of an alphabet are arranged in horizontal rows under the numbers 1–9.

1	2	3	4	5	6	7	8	9
A	B	C	D	E	F	G	H	I
J	K	L	M	N	O	P	Q	R
S	T	U	V	W	X	Y	Z	

In this book, as we explore how Cosmic Numerology can be used for healing, we will use this conversion chart to transpose the letters of an illness, disease, or injury into their numeric equivalents. The conversion chart is also used to identify karmic lessons, which are determined by which letters (and numbers) have been omitted from an individual's name. Looking at the relationship between a person's numbers and the illness or disease he or she may have contracted/ created, I have found that the patterns show an almost direct relationship between the individual's numeric challenges and the numbers of the illness or disease.

THE MATH

When you add the numeric total of all the letters in a word or series of words, you will usually get a multi-digit number. You will also often get a two-digit number when adding the numbers of a birth date. The individual numbers that make up a two- or three-digit number identify the underlying energies of a name, behavior, illness, or injury. The numbers are always reduced to a single digit but are written with the two- and/ or three-digit number as well. Let's look at an example: The numeric total for the word *indigestion* is 62. To reduce the word to a single digit, we add the 6 + 2 to get a sum of 8. The numbers for indigestion are written as 62/8.

Practice converting a few words into their numeric equivalents and then use the following section to see how the positive and negative interpretations of the numbers match the energy of the words. For example, *love* adds up to 18, is reduced to 9 (1 + 8 = 9), and is written as 18/9. *True love,* a positive 9, deals with selflessness. Negative 9 would be *egotistical* (see page 20).

The letter-to-number conversion and figuring the numeric totals are vital concepts to grasp, as the descriptions of the illnesses and diseases are mostly written as two- or three-digit numbers reduced to a single digit (i.e., Fibromyalgia 64/10/1, which is written as 64/1).

POSITIVE AND NEGATIVE INTERPRETATIONS
OF THE NUMBERS

Positive and negative particles of energy flow harmoniously through the universe and our bodies' systems. They are the energies of creation. I believe that the proportion of negative energy particles to positive particles in our etheric and physical bodies increases in direct proportion to the intensity of our abandonment issues. Repetitive negative responses to environmental stimuli trigger negative responses in our physical, mental, emotional, and etheric bodies—the manifestation of illness or disease.

Every number is composed of both positive and negative energy. In this instance, the terms *positive* and *negative* are being used to describe the flow of energetic patterns of choice and not as things that are either *good* or *bad*. Living the positive aspects of a number enables one to lead a more proactive and less reactive life.

The following summary of each number's theme and principal positive and negative qualities will be helpful to refer back to as a reminder throughout the book. Take the time to learn the positive and negative interpretations of the numbers 1–9; they will greatly assist you in understanding the nuances of your behavior patterns. When first learning the interpretations for each number, start by focusing on the main theme—for example, the number 1 involves "Issues of the Ego Self" and the number 2 "Communication and Interaction with Others." Once you recognize your behavior patterns, you can choose to change them and create a healthier life by practicing the positive aspects of your numeric daisy chains (which will be explained in chapter 4). It will take time to understand how all of the numbers and pieces of this practice fit together. To begin with, just look at the numbers as energetic catalysts for your illness or disease. As you analyze the numeric aspects of your illness or disease (in chapter 5), study all of the negative aspects of the numbers that compose that illness or disease and determine which apply to you and

18   How Cosmic Numerology Works

```
1 2 3 4 5 6 7 8 9
A B C D E F G H I
J K L M N O P Q R
S T U V W X Y Z
```

have direct correspondences to your various challenge numbers (which you will find in chapter 3). If you would like more information on the interpretation of all of your numbers and how they fit together, you may want to get a basic numerology book to enhance your understanding of the material in this book (see Recommended Reading).

1 • Issues of the Ego Self

Positive: Self-directed, leader, paradigm buster, innovator, assertive, energetic, balanced, follows internal guidance, an initiator, comfortable with self

Negative: Passive, aggressive, egocentric, low self-esteem, fearful, timid, arrogant, a zealot, a bully, no sense of self

2 • Issues Involving Communication and Interaction with Others

Positive: Sensitive, intuitive, cooperative, a mediator/arbitrator, friendly, communicates in timely fashion, detail oriented, tactful, loyal, an organizer and harmonizer

Negative: Subservient, shy, overly sentimental, timid, careless about "things," codependent, does not speak up for self, self-centered, has difficulty releasing emotional and sentimental attachments, blunt, insensitive, has difficulty working with others—not a team player—hides emotions

3 • Issues Involving Social Interactions and Acceptance of Self and Others

Positive: Joyful, witty, artistic, charismatic, charming, creative, intelligent, optimistic, communicator, extrovert, visionary, musician, good sense of humor—likes to laugh

Negative: Moody/emotional, unforgiving, scattered, introvert, exaggerates, vain, feelings of inferiority or inadequacy, leaves things unfinished, sarcastic, grandiose plans, jealousy, overly concerned about being judged, temperamental, ill-tempered

4 • Issues Involving "Getting It Done": Procrastination, Control, and Constrictions

Positive: Organized, architect, builder, systematic, logical, dependable, practical, manager, ability to focus totally on a task, a logician, reliable, has a natural feel for order, system, and structure

Negative: Prejudicial, a reactionary, a procrastinator, unimaginative, gets lost in minutiae, stubborn, goes by his or her "book," confrontational, dull, hides in logic, can be hateful

5 • Issues Involving Change and Movement

Positive: Flexible, freedom loving, physical, enjoys life, loves innovation and change, curious, can be moderate, balanced

Negative: Rigid, impulsive, self-indulgent, inconsistent, promiscuous, physical excesses, too yielding, unbalanced

6 • Issues Involving Responsibility to Family, Community, and Relationships

Positive: Responsible, adviser/counselor, protector, nurturer, humanitarian, service oriented, domestic, compassionate

Negative: Perfectionist, martyr, nosy, overly protective, a giver of unsought advice, difficulty making commitments, codependent, irresponsible—avoids obligations, commitments, relationships, or responsibility

7 • Issues Involving Trust, Skepticism, and Control

Positive: Trusting, spiritual, analytical, psychic, introspective, empathic, objective, open, vulnerable, a seeker of knowledge, patient, insightful, analytical, can see all sides of an issue

Negative: Controlling, fearful, distrustful, impatient, a need to be needed, emotionally closed, mental or emotional paralysis from being overly analytical, totally disconnected emotionally, zealot, martyr, messianic feelings, codependent

```
1 2 3 4 5 6 7 8 9
A B C D E F G H I
J K L M N O P Q R
S T U V W X Y Z
```

20   How Cosmic Numerology Works

8 • Issues Involving Power, Money, Control, and Status

Positive: Initiates/delegates/orchestrates, logical, likes to be in charge, a leader, makes it happen, good at politics or business and commerce or leading institutions and organizations, "walks the talk"

Negative: Easily frustrated, temperamental, extravagant/cheap, dictatorial, stubborn, materialistic, demands recognition, mean, a bully, fearful of using personal power, can be disloyal if he or she feels slighted or ignored

9 • Issues Involving Selflessness

Positive: Selfless, loves unconditionally, compassionate, brotherhood, a natural actor, loves long-distance travel, comfortable with all strata of society, works to raise the level of self-awareness on the planet, has let go of ego issues and embraced the higher Self

Negative: Egotistical, needs recognition/appreciation/thanks for his or her "good deeds," has difficulty letting go, can be fearful of showing any emotion, can be emotionally isolated or codependent, can be an "emotional pin cushion" (i.e., holds the emotions and feelings of others as a reservoir holds water)

0 • Issues Related to Spirit

The zero (0) is the combination of the nine separate energies. A zero attached to any number indicates *direct* spiritual assistance with that energy. For example, the number 10 indicates assistance with endeavors involving beginnings and leadership. The number 102 could indicate assistance in individual projects (1) that would be of benefit to others (2).

3

Finding Your
Challenge Numbers

The challenges fall into three main categories: the achievement number, major and minor life challenges, and karmic lessons. The illnesses and diseases we are most prone to manifest are those that match the numbers of our various challenges. While working with this chapter and learning how to find your personal numbers, practice the formulas on a piece of scrap paper.

THE ACHIEVEMENT NUMBER

I believe the achievement number is the most important number in your recipe; it flavors every other number.* This number represents the prime challenge of your life. It is the hub of your numerological wheel from which other numbers radiate like spokes. As we will see in chapter 4, it determines your negative behavior tendencies in relation to all

---

*Although I've never seen it in a copyrighted format, to the best of my knowledge the achievement number concept was initially developed by Kevin Quinn Avery. I have adapted and simplified the process.

of your personal numbers and is the key number for determining right action.

Until you become aware of and resolve the issues associated with your achievement number, its negative aspects rule your life. For example, if your achievement number is a 3, you must learn to finish what you start by overcoming feelings of insecurity, inadequacy, and inferiority. Whether it's flipping pancakes or performing brain surgery, if you feel/know in your heart that you're the best at what you do and love doing it, then the feelings of inadequacy and insecurity associated with the 3 will dissolve.

Since, as we have already discussed, abandonment issues are the root cause of negative behavior patterns and thus illnesses and diseases, I'd like to take a moment to ask you a question: Is there *anything* in this universe that has the exact same molecular structure as you? The answer is no. If there is nothing else like you in the universe, you must be unique. If you are unique, then whatever you do, as long as you are doing your best, you are the best in the universe at what you are doing. If you can accept this thought, you can eliminate all insecurity from your life. If you can believe you are the best at what you do, then you will no longer need to be validated by others. If you can own this concept, you can eliminate the driving need to be thanked, recognized, loved, or appreciated. You can also eliminate the need to maintain control of everything and thus eliminate a chief source of stress from your life.

Every challenge has a soulution (to be discussed in greater detail in chapter 4). What's most interesting about the soulution to the achievement number is that regardless of which of the nine achievement numbers you have chosen for yourself, the soulution for every achievement challenge is the number 9. *The soulution is to always act and think for the highest good of all by doing what you love and what gives you the greatest joy.* The soulution of 9 also indicates that we can overcome the ego's fears of abandonment by learning to communicate with our divine self (the soul), thereby overcoming the fear that we are alone, unloved,

1	2	3	4	5	6	7	8	9
A	B	C	D	E	F	G	H	I
J	K	L	M	N	O	P	Q	R
S	T	U	V	W	X	Y	Z	

Finding Your Challenge Numbers **23**

and abandoned and that existence on Earth is punishment for some unknown action we can't remember. Our soul never forgets its connection with the God energy. We consciously decided to enter this dimension and the earth realm at this time to complete our divine mission. We did not come here to be in pain, experience loneliness, or "screw up." We came to do what we love most . . . fulfill our life calling.

The prescription for healing yourself is to follow your heart, not your head. To do this, you need to do what you love and stop "doing" to be loved or to maintain control. Then, thank your spiritual trainers for helping you develop your inner strength. Finally, make yourself your first priority. Start with the next new moon—a time for planting. Plant the seeds for the new you by marrying yourself. Make up your own words or use the words for a traditional marriage ceremony. Invite

Notes on Using Your Achievement Number

- Whatever number you are interpreting, whether it is associated with your name, soul, destiny, life's work, health, or any other aspect of your numerological chart, always consider the influence of the achievement number. Remember, this number not only determines the challenges you will face, along with their soulutions, but it is the base ingredient of your numerological recipe as well and therefore flavors everything else.
- Imagine the achievement number as a mirror that reflects back your positive and negative qualities.
- If the achievement number appears as part of another number, pay particular attention to that number, as it presents an opportunity for rapid growth via a challenge. For example, if you have an achievement number of 3, pay particular attention to any other number with a three (3, 12/3, 23/5, 33/6, 53/8, etc.) whether it's another challenge number or the number of a disease or illness.

over some friends or perform this ceremony alone. What's important is that you commit to making yourself your first priority. This is not about becoming selfish but about becoming self-full. Being self-full will allow you to radiate your energy like a star, instead of being like a pond that can be drained. Becoming self-full will allow you to transform your achievement number from your core challenge to your greatest strength.

How to Determine Your Achievement Number

Note: When figuring your achievement number, use the birth date on your birth certificate or the date of your court-approved name change.

To determine your achievement number, add together the numbers for your month and day of birth. Write down the sum. If the number is a double digit, write the sum of those two numbers following the original sum. Let's look at a few examples:

> If your birthday is March 4, add together 3 + 4 for an achievement number of 7.
>
> If your birthday is February 25, add together 2 + 25 for a sum of 27. Reduce the 27 by adding together 2 + 7 for an achievement number of 9. The number is written as 27/9.
>
> October 8 would be 10 + 8 = 18 and 1 + 8 = 9. Your achievement number is 9.

Add the numbers together until you get a single digit. For example:

If your birthday is December 26: 12 + 26 = 38, 3 + 8 = 11, and 1 + 1 = 2. You would then write your achievement number as 38/2.

The two-digit numbers are treated this way because their energy determines additional influences affecting the interpretation of the single digit. A 38/2 is an achievement number of 2; however, the 8 shows a tendency to avoid accepting personal empowerment because of feelings of inadequacy (associated with the number 3) or being a bully who is sarcastic or insensitive in dealing with others. The 38/2 will therefore have different meaning from a 29/2.

In addition to the numbers 1–9, the master numbers (11, 22, 33, and multiples of 11 through 99) and the karmic numbers (13, 14, 16, 19) are listed as achievement numbers in the following section. If you have a karmic or master number in your birth date equation (for instance, with May 17, 5 + 17 = 22), read the interpretation for that number in addition to the interpretation of its reduced, single digit (for example, 22 = 4, 13 = 4, 19 = 1, etc.).

INTERPRETATIONS OF THE ACHIEVEMENT NUMBERS

The following descriptions of the achievement numbers encompass both extremes of behavior patterns—that is, having too much or too little of some aspect of the self. Once the negative aspects of the achievement number are recognized and resolved, this number will become your greatest strength and you will embody the positive qualities of the number, which are repeated following each achievement number description.

1 • Self-esteem is the main issue. You must learn to stand on your own and not to let others define your identity or make your decisions. Have the courage and faith that what you feel in your heart is the right course of action. Lack of self-esteem can also lead to arrogance and bullying others.

   Positive: Self-directed, leader, paradigm buster, innovator, assertive, energetic, balanced, follows internal guidance, an initiator, comfortable with self

2 • Oversensitivity, timidity, fear, and shyness are the main issues. Do not base your identity on the perceptions of others. Let go of things much sooner than you now do (you hold on for emotional or sentimental reasons). Pay attention to details. Practice tact, cooperation, and getting along with feminine energy (anyone, male

or female, coming from their hearts instead of their heads). Speak up in a timely manner. If you don't have difficulty speaking up, then put more padding on the end of your hammer as you shatter people's illusions. Listen to your intuition.

In some women and possibly men too, this inability to speak up or to express themselves may be one cause of curvature of the spine. The trapped emotions begin to pull and tug at the spine, causing it to bend or twist. It may also be an underlying cause of stiff/sore necks, back pain, upper respiratory problems, and sore throats.

Positive: Sensitive, intuitive, cooperative, a mediator/arbitrator, friendly, communicates in timely fashion, detail oriented, tactful, loyal, an organizer and harmonizer

3 • Overcoming feelings of insecurity, inferiority, or inadequacy are the main issues. You can dazzle people with your creativity, charm, charisma, and intelligence, but you don't always finish what you start because you don't want to be judged. (If you were given a dime each time someone told you what "great potential" you have, you could retire!) The soulution is to master something, anything, and to finish what you start. It doesn't matter if it's cleaning houses, riding a bike, being a homemaker, a mechanic, or a brain surgeon. To overcome those feelings of inadequacy, you need to feel and believe that you are the best at what you do. Learn to communicate well, either orally or in writing, and watch the sarcasm. Be more forgiving of yourself and others.

Positive: Joyful, witty, artistic, charismatic, charming, creative, intelligent, optimistic, communicator, extrovert, visionary, musician, good sense of humor—likes to laugh

4 • You like order, system, and structure. At the extreme, you would carry a red pen to correct the grammar or spelling on commercial signs. Don't be overly logical and get stuck in the minutiae of going "by the book" (your book). You could be confrontational with

authority, as you feel you should be the boss. The main challenges are to build a solid foundation, not to take shortcuts or procrastinate, and not to be judgmental, stubborn, or prejudicial.

Positive: Organized, architect, builder, systematic, logical, dependable, practical, manager, ability to totally focus on a task, a logician, reliable

5 • At times, you can be so flexible and bend over so far backward for people that you have to pick cinders out of the back of your head. At other times, you are so rigid that you need to have someone put liniment on your back so that you can get out of bed. You must learn to be moderate in all actions (mental, physical, emotional, and spiritual) and to go with the flow when dealing with change. There will always be a *go slow/go fast, too little/too much* quality involving the physical plane. Learn moderation of the senses.

Positive: Flexible, freedom loving, physical, enjoys life, loves innovation and change, curious, can be moderate, balanced

6 • You like to be the "cosmic mother or father," yet you don't want the responsibility unless you are given the authority because you don't want to take the heat for someone else's mistakes. Your challenge is to learn to accept responsibility, first for yourself, and then to responsibly be of service to family and community. Don't be an emotional buffer for others. Ease out of your perfectionistic tendencies. Health issues may involve the stomach and intestinal areas, and be caused by being too emotionally involved.

Positive: Responsible, adviser/counselor, protector, nurturer, humanitarian, service oriented, domestic, compassionate

7 • Overcome your need to be the teacher or healer, advising or telling others what they need to do (thinking you'll help them avoid pain and suffering). It only creates frustration for you when they don't listen and feeds into your sense of being different or isolated. Above

1	2	3	4	5	6	7	8	9
A	B	C	D	E	F	G	H	I
J	K	L	M	N	O	P	Q	R
S	T	U	V	W	X	Y	Z	

28 Finding Your Challenge Numbers

all else, you must learn faith and patience. Trust that the universe unfolds according to the divine plan. You must learn to subjugate your personal agendas and allow the universe to unfold before you. Stop being overly analytical. Also, you must never engage in purposeless activity—doing something just because you are bored—it will lead to negative consequences. Emotionally, you find it very hard to open up and be vulnerable. It's much easier for you to give than to receive.

Positive: Trusting, spiritual, analytical, psychic, introspective, empathic, objective, open, vulnerable, a seeker of knowledge, patient, insightful, analytical, can see all sides of an issue

8 • You can spend money like a drunken sailor or squeeze a dollar so hard that tears come to George's eyes. You can become frustrated if you feel you are not being given the recognition you believe you deserve. This may lead to disloyalty on your part. Stop demanding recognition . . . walk the walk, don't just talk the talk. Learn to deal with authority, even though you feel you should be in charge. Don't try to do it all yourself; learn to delegate to others. Develop true humanitarian feelings. Don't depend just on your logic; learn to trust your intuition as well.

Positive: Initiates/delegates/orchestrates, logical, likes to be in charge, a leader, makes it happen, good at politics or business and commerce and leading institutions or organizations, "walks the talk"

9 • When 9 is your achievement number, it indicates that you can be an "emotional pincushion," as you have a tendency to absorb and internalize other people's pain and suffering. This can lead to the possibility of lower back pain and/or stiffness in the neck area between the shoulders. You are here to learn to deal with your emotions; be more compassionate; use your life experiences to help heal others; let go of the past and start new; give of yourself with no thought of recognition, appreciation, or thanks; do for others

before doing for yourself; and to learn to "be in the world, but not of it" by practicing unconditional love. Souls selecting 9 for their achievement number have chosen to speed up their return Home by dealing with multiple issues in a short period of time. This can make life very intense, as the 9 achievement number also encompasses the lessons of the eight numbers that precede it.

Positive: Selfless, loves unconditionally, compassionate, brotherhood, a natural actor, loves long-distance travel, comfortable with all strata of society, works to raise the level of self-awareness on the planet, has let go of ego issues and embraced the higher self

Master Numbers

11 • The first of the master numbers (11, 22, 33, etc.), 11 is also the most frustrating. Under the influence of this number, you can see the way things ought to be but are not given the power or opportunity to make them that way. People born in November or on the eleventh of any month have a tendency to beat up on themselves. This master number can bring a sense of self-righteousness and hypersensitivity. It brings knowledge of how things ought to be and a frustration that you cannot make them so. It also carries the same vibrations as the 2 achievement number.

Positive: Sensitive, intuitive, cooperative, a mediator/arbitrator, friendly, communicates in a timely fashion, detail oriented, tactful, loyal, an organizer and harmonizer

22 • This master number can make relationships a bit difficult, as there is a sense that the universe has selected you to accomplish some grand plan—you just don't know what it is. It can also indicate grandiose plans that never come to fruition because of procrastination and a need for preapproval. For example, you may point out to your manager a unique way of doing something that could make your company large profits. The manager asks you to write up your proposal, but you want a guarantee that the plan will be

implemented and that you will receive due credit. The manager says, "I can't guarantee anything. Write the plan." You hesitate because you don't like to waste your energy. If there is no guarantee, you don't want to put forth effort that won't be rewarded. Yet people can't reward you because they have no plan to comment upon. It's a vicious circle. Remember, it's just as important for people to know what they don't want as it is for them to know what they do want, and they won't know either until they see the options, so put your idea out there! You can be a great organizer. Work on cooperation and compromise as well as your communication skills. Learn to use the words *"If we modify"* rather than *"We need to change."* As you well know, when we are asked to "change" something we've put together, we become defensive. This number also carries the characteristics of the 4 achievement number.

Positive: As a master builder you can put tunnels through mountains, run a multinational company, start your own religion, or build cities. There is nothing you cannot do if you pay attention to the details and don't get lost in them. The positive aspect of this number leads to not waiting for the preapproval of others to implement ideas or visions. This number also carries the positive characteristics of the 4 achievement number.

33 • With the 33 achievement number, you can be either a master teacher or healer or a master martyr. The challenge with this master number is to avoid being overly involved emotionally in the lives of others. You also need to learn to stop sacrificing yourself for others to the point of martyrdom. The 33 calls for distancing yourself from emotional entanglements that cause you pain because you can't help or your advice is ignored. The 33 requires you to move toward compassion. Compassion allows you to be empathic, to feel without being a part of the pain. This number also carries the characteristics of the 6 achievement number.

Positive: Responsible, adviser/counselor, protector, nurturer, humanitarian, service oriented, domestic, compassionate

Karmic Numbers

Note: Wherever a karmic number (13, 14, 16, 19) appears—be it in an achievement number, a major or minor life challenge, a karmic lesson, or as the numbers for an illness—its energy will always be the same.

13 • A karmic number that indicates laziness in past lives; the individual did not apply him/herself and let others do more than their share. It also indicates a reticence in transitioning from past to future. There is difficulty, if not outright refusal, to accept advice from others. Imagine this—you walk into a room of twenty people and know everyone by her first name. Out of the corner of your eye, you see a sign that says WET PAINT. You look at the group and the group simultaneously says, "It's wet!" You say, "I know that." You then surreptitiously go over to the painted wall and gently touch it. You look at the paint on your fingers, then look at the group and say, "Yup, it's wet!" A 13 can also be associated with feelings of inadequacy (3) and low self-esteem (1), which can make people procrastinate or be extremely stubborn. This number also carries the characteristics of the 4 achievement number.

Positive: An innovative (1) visionary (3) capable of making dreams into reality. Organized, architect, builder, systematic, logical, dependable, practical, natural manager, ability to totally focus on a task, a logician, reliable

14 • A karmic number that indicates excessive behaviors in the area of physical desires (food, drugs, drink, sex, gambling, etc.). With the 14, if some is good, more is better! This is an energy that can lead to stretching the boundaries. Negative 14s can be either stubborn (4) due to low self-esteem (1) or be very impulsive, not paying attention to the details (4) only the concepts (5)—a "me first" attitude. This

32 Finding Your Challenge Numbers

1	2	3	4	5	6	7	8	9
A	B	C	D	E	F	G	H	I
J	K	L	M	N	O	P	Q	R
S	T	U	V	W	X	Y	Z	

number also carries the characteristics of the 5 achievement number.

Positive: Flexible, freedom loving, physical, enjoys life, loves innovation and change, curious, can be moderate, balanced, accepts the transitory nature of life

16 • A karmic number that indicates the possibility of catastrophe or loss if the cosmic "law of right action" (listening to your heart) is not followed. If 16 is your achievement number, you have a tendency to follow your head and not your heart—to play by your own rules out of fear that things will not work the way they are supposed to and you will be embarrassed. For example, you go to buy a used car and a voice inside says, "Pass it up." You ignore the voice because you like the color of the car or the stereo system or you don't want to appear to be wasting the salesperson's time. You buy the car and it turns out to be a lemon. The 16 also indicates being overly concerned about the welfare of others and jumping into their lives because you believe your advice can save them pain and suffering. You then feel hurt and unappreciated when they reject your unsolicited advice. Stop trying to put square pegs in round holes! Even though you are right 99 percent of the time, you are not right 100 percent of the time. Therefore, you cannot "tell" people what they ought to be doing. Your own abandonment issues drive you to be needed and thus validated by others. You are not a messiah; you have your own soul-chosen direction. Until you learn to replace your agendas with preferences and personal control with a divine partnership, life could be difficult. This number also carries the characteristics of the 7 achievement number.

Positive: Trusting, spiritual, analytical, psychic, introspective, empathic, objective, open, vulnerable, a seeker of knowledge, patient, insightful, analytical, can see all sides of an issue

19 • A karmic number that indicates ongoing work on balancing the masculine (1) and feminine (9) energies. For example, on Monday,

1	2	3	4	5	6	7	8	9
A	B	C	D	E	F	G	H	I
J	K	L	M	N	O	P	Q	R
S	T	U	V	W	X	Y	Z	

Finding Your Challenge Numbers **33**

Wednesday, and Friday you can be like Mother Teresa—loving, compassionate, philanthropic. On Tuesday, Thursday, and Saturday, you can be like Genghis Khan—off with their heads! Then, one day in the week, you manage to balance both sides of yourself. The 19 brings with it some pain and suffering (especially in the first twenty years of life) that can lead to compassionate behavior and a stronger sense of self. There could be a tendency to be argumentative with authority figures. This number also carries the characteristics of the 1 achievement number.

Positive: Self-directed, leader, paradigm buster, innovator, assertive, energetic, balanced, follows internal guidance, an initiator, comfortable with self

LIFE CHALLENGE NUMBERS

Most people have three life challenge numbers; some have four. These challenges, rooted in personality and emotion, can be lifelong or may peak at certain times. Life challenges are divided into major and minor challenges. The major challenge represents an aspect of your personality that you need to work on daily. The two minor challenges are most active during specific subcycles (influencing your mental processes) and pinnacles (describing the cycle of physical events in your life). If they are not recognized and worked on, they can linger under the surface throughout your life, especially if the same numbers appear elsewhere among your challenge or other personal numbers. Occasionally, there can be a third minor challenge, different from the other two. I call this a "minor-major" challenge. Like the major challenge, this challenge is active throughout life.

The personal numbers (derived from the numeric sums of your name and birth day) that activate your life challenges are the catalysts for your unresolved issues, reveal major challenges to the personality, and are symbiotic with the achievement number.

> ## Notes on Using Your Life Challenge Numbers
>
> - If a life challenge number appears as part of any other number, pay particular attention to that number, as it presents an opportunity to resolve negative aspects of the personality. For example, if you have a major or minor life challenge of 1, pay particular attention to any number with a one (1, 17/8, 21/3, 37/1, 41/5, etc.), whether it's another challenge number or the number of a disease or illness.
> - If the major life challenge number is the same as the achievement number, a karmic lesson, or both, this individual has decided to accelerate his spiritual growth by resolving a particular issue he has avoided dealing with throughout several lifetimes. This can make this life very challenging in specific areas.

HOW TO DETERMINE YOUR LIFE CHALLENGE NUMBERS

Note: When figuring your life challenge numbers, use the birth date on your birth certificate, unless you legally changed your name (for a reason other than marriage), in which case you should use the date the court approved the name change.

The life challenge numbers are determined by a subtraction formula that uses the month, day, and year of birth. The smaller number is always subtracted from the larger number. If subtracting two numbers gives you a 0, change the 0 to a 9. (It's a long story—trust me, it works!)

Prior to using the following subtraction formulas, reduce the numbers of the month, day, and year of birth to single digits. Let's look at an example using the birth date of October 20, 1949. The month of October corresponds to the number 10, which is reduced to a 1 by adding 1 + 0; likewise, the 20th day is reduced to a 2. The year 1949 is reduced to 23 by adding 1 + 9 + 4 + 9. The 23 is reduced further by adding 2 + 3, which gives us 5. For this example, then, the month number is 1, the day number is 2, and the year number is 5.

Once you have reduced the numbers of your birth date to single digits, you are ready to discover your life challenge numbers.

Minor Challenge 1: Using the single-digit numbers, subtract the number for your birth month from the day of birth (or vice versa, depending on which is the larger number). Using our example of 10/20/1949, we subtract 1 (month) from 2 (day) for a minor challenge of 1.

This minor challenge number is most active from birth through the age of thirty-five.

Minor Challenge 2: Again using the single-digit numbers, find the difference between the day of birth and the year of birth. Using our example, we subtract 2 (day) from 5 (year) for a second minor challenge of 3.

This minor challenge number is most active from age thirty-six through fifty.

Major Challenge: To find your major challenge number, subtract the two minor challenge numbers from each other. The 1 (first minor challenge) subtracted from the 3 (second minor challenge) gives us a major challenge of 2.

The major challenge number is active throughout your time on Earth; it is a lifelong challenge but may be especially active throughout the forties.

Minor-Major Challenge: To determine if there is a fourth challenge that is numerically different from the other three, find the difference between the single-digit numbers for the month and year of birth. If this number is different from the other three life challenge numbers, it is a minor-major, lifelong challenge. Using our example, 5 (year) minus 1 (month) gives us a minor-major challenge of 4.

Remember, if the answer to any of these equations is 0, convert the 0 to a 9.

INTERPRETATIONS OF THE LIFE CHALLENGE NUMBERS

One or more aspects of the following interpretations may apply to a life challenge number.

1 • Passive-aggressive, a bully, egocentric, low self-esteem, weak willed, a follower, has a need to initiate in order to maintain control

2 • Shy, overly emotional or sentimental, has difficulty letting go of emotional or sentimental attachments, timid, careless about things and details, may not speak up in a timely fashion, may be overly brusque, difficulty cooperating or compromising, insensitive, ignores intuition, could become codependent, may have "sticky" fingers

3 • Moody/emotional, unforgiving, scattered (lack of focus), introverted, exaggerates, braggart, vain, feelings of inferiority/insecurity/inadequacy, nonsocial

4 • Prejudicial, procrastinator, not very imaginative, gets lost in the details, stubborn, overly logical, wants to go "by the book," inability to concentrate, confrontational with authority, controlling, workaholic, highly opinionated

5 • Rigid, impulsive, self-indulgent, inconsistent, promiscuous, prone to physical excesses, high-strung, fearful of change, fearful of the physical world, restless, overly flexible

6 • Perfectionist (also, if he can't do something "right," he won't do it at all), a martyr, nosy, overly protective, irresponsible, unable to connect with family/friends or community, a need to be loved, could

substitute sweets or food for love, wants everyone to be "happy" (by her definition of happiness)

7 • Controlling, faithless, fearful, non-trusting, a need to be needed, emotionally closed, overly analytical, detached, perfectionist, non-involvement, doesn't honor intuitive/psychic feelings, overly dependent on logic, hides vulnerability, impatient

8 • Frustration/anger/temper, extravagant/stingy, dictatorial, stubborn, materialistic, overly logical, demands recognition, can be disloyal, abuses power, materialistic, pompous, fears the material world and its requirements, confrontational, self-centered, has grandiose ideas, a bully

9 • Egotistical, expects recognition/appreciation/thanks for deeds, cannot let go emotionally, overly sentimental, overly dramatic, overly attached, an emotional sponge, lack of concern for others, selfish. Also contains elements of each of the other eight challenges.

KARMIC LESSONS

Karmic lessons are determined by the soul's conscious omission of specific letters from its name, whether it's a birth name, adopted name, or a name that has been legally changed (for reasons other than marriage). These challenges, if not resolved, are carried forth from one life to the next.

HOW TO DETERMINE YOUR KARMIC LESSONS

Using the conversion chart, identify the letters missing from your name. Write down your full name and place the corresponding number under each letter of the name. The numbers that are missing represent the karmic lessons to be learned.

For example, in my name, Michael Richard Brill, the numbers 6 and 7 are not present. The missing letters *F, O,* and *X* represent the

1	2	3	4	5	6	7	8	9
A	B	C	D	E	F	G	H	I
J	K	L	M	N	O	P	Q	R
S	T	U	V	W	X	Y	Z	

38   Finding Your Challenge Numbers

number 6 and the missing letters *G, P,* and *Y* represent the number 7. My name reveals two karmic lessons: 6 and 7.

M I C H A E L   R I C H A R D   B R I L L

4 9 3 8 1 5 3   9 9 3 8 1 9 4   2 9 9 3 3 = No 6 or 7

Notes on Using Your Karmic Lessons

• If each number is accounted for, it indicates that there are no karmic lessons to learn in this lifetime. However, if this is the case, you have chosen to work on some particular aspect of yourself, so look for the frequency with which numbers occur. For example, in a name that has one 1, three 2s, one 3, two 4s, one 5, one 6, two 7s, one 8, and four 9s, there are more single occurrences of a number (one each of 1, 3, 5, 6, and 8) than any other combination. This indicates having chosen to refine issues revolving around the number 1 (ego and self) in this lifetime. The interpretation of this number (see the negative interpretations for this number on page 18) will reveal a hidden and subtle life challenge.

• If a karmic lesson number also appears as part of any other number (especially the achievement number or a life challenge number), pay particular attention to that number wherever it appears; it presents an opportunity to resolve karma in that area. For example, if you have an achievement number and karmic lesson of 7 (indicating fear, impatience, control, and vulnerability issues), pay particular attention to any number with a seven (17/8, 27/9, 37/1, 47/2, 127/1, etc.), whether it's another challenge number or the number of an illness or disease.

1	2	3	4	5	6	7	8	9
A	B	C	D	E	F	G	H	I
J	K	L	M	N	O	P	Q	R
S	T	U	V	W	X	Y	Z

Finding Your Challenge Numbers **39**

INTERPRETATIONS OF THE KARMIC LESSONS

1 • This number rarely appears as a karmic lesson. When it does, it indicates a personality that has avoided making decisions or assuming leadership roles. Being weak-willed, you model yourself on others. In this lifetime, you will be presented with opportunities to assume a strong identity, to rely on your own judgment, and to form your own opinions. You may be required to fight for your rights and your place in life. If you appear arrogant, it is only the flip side of timidity; you are still insecure.

2 • In the past, you have avoided cooperating, compromising, and/ or being sensitive to the thoughts and feeling of others. You were overly concerned with yourself and were generally short on patience and tact. In this lifetime, you will be given opportunities to be of service, pay attention to details, make sacrifices for the highest good of the group, and learn diplomacy and loyalty.

3 • In the past, you have failed to learn to express yourself because of a lack of confidence. You can be easily intimidated and allow others to stifle your creativity and self-expression. As a result, you try to avoid being noticed and, therefore, minimize your contact with people. Stop apologizing and holding your breath! In this lifetime, you will be given opportunities to speak up, socialize, and be involved with the public (most likely in some type of sales or service). Lift up your eyes, unfold your arms from across your chest, and embrace life!

4 • Your motto may still be "I'd like to retire before I get in the habit of working for a living!" In the past, you have felt that physical labor was beneath you and performed only by those with lesser mental abilities. Well, it doesn't matter whether you are digging a sewage trench, shuffling papers, or performing brain surgery. To be successful requires physical labor. In this lifetime, you will be given

1	2	3	4	5	6	7	8	9
A	B	C	D	E	F	G	H	I
J	K	L	M	N	O	P	Q	R
S	T	U	V	W	X	Y	Z	

40 Finding Your Challenge Numbers

opportunities to overcome procrastination. Whether you get lost in the details or avoid the task completely, it's still procrastination. You need to learn self-discipline and establish order and structure in your life.

5 • This number rarely appears as a karmic lesson. When it does, it can indicate a fear of life. You have a fear of the unknown and of being required to change. This can lead to trying to repress those around you. You can be very rigid, intolerant, antisocial, and close-minded. In this lifetime, you will be forced to accept change in people, places, and things. You will frequently encounter the unexpected, possibly even crises, to make you more flexible. You may find that you are living in a vortex of change: relationships can be fleeting, work can be a roller coaster, and even finding a place to settle into may be difficult until you learn the lessons of tolerance, flexibility, versatility, and agreeableness.

6 • This lesson makes relationships difficult. In the past, you were so wrapped up in yourself that you wanted no part of unions, partnerships, obligations, close relationships, or personal responsibility. You were never devoted to anything but yourself and knew nothing about being of service or lending a helping hand to others. In this lifetime, until you learn to accept responsibility and be of service to others, obligations will be forced upon you, often creating emotional, physical, or financial hardships. Learn to do your "duty" and do it with love. There is the possibility of at least one divorce—whether it involves the breakup of a long-term relationship or an actual legal divorce—unless you learn the lesson of being a good partner and creating a loving family/home environment. People will expect much from you and you will receive little in return—this is another test. It is very important that you finish whatever you start.

7 • This is one of the most frequently occurring karmic lessons. It deals with fear—the fear of embarrassment or humiliation due to a mistake; the fear of not being "religious" enough (you need to learn the difference between spirituality and religion); the irrational fear that others will discover you are a fake and throw you to the lions! These fears cause you to be overly logical, distrustful, and have multiple plans for every situation. By golly, you'll not be caught off guard! You'll be prepared for a thousand variations! But it doesn't work like that. The lesson here is to go within, face your fears, and develop faith. Each day, you need to make time to review the events of the day and decide what you accomplished, what you avoided, what you screwed up—then decide what you want to work on tomorrow. Get out of your head and learn to feel what is important through your heart, the doorway through which your soul speaks to you. Become more vulnerable by opening your heart, knowing everything is divinely perfect.

8 • In past lives, you have avoided making decisions, handling money, managing your own affairs, or assuming a position of authority. You have also avoided the business and commercial world because you are afraid of failure or criticism. Until you learn to make decisions, use good judgment, and participate in the world of commerce, life will be frustrating and, at times, disappointing. Money has always been hard to come by and, when it does show up, it's always needed for unexpected expenses. For example, you win $500 on a scratch-and-win lottery ticket. You go to bed with a smile. It snows during the night and as a car comes around the corner near your house, it skids on the ice and hits your parked car. You have a $500 deductible on your insurance policy—there goes your $500. Once you get it all together and stand at the door of prosperity and abundance, the most important thing to remember is never to use your wealth, power, or status strictly

for personal gain. If you do, there is the distinct probability that you will lose everything—your health, your possessions, your happiness—as 8 is also the number of karma, which comes into play when we are unable to complete our lessons in a given lifetime.

9 • This number rarely appears as a karmic lesson. It indicates that in past lives you put your emotions in a bottle and sealed it shut. In this lifetime, you are to learn to give with no expectations of thanks, recognition, or appreciation. You are to learn to let go of egocentric behavior patterns and fears, to learn compassion, empathy, love, and selflessness. You have chosen to be a human on this planet, and to be human entails dealing with and growing through your emotions and feelings. Since you have refused to do this voluntarily in the past, in this lifetime you will grow through experiencing pain and heartache. Until you can love selflessly, a loving relationship will elude you. Your mission this time around is to give selflessly and unconditionally.

ADDITIONAL INSIGHTS

The following list includes additional information that can be derived from names and birth dates. This information is not expanded on further in this text but you now have all of the tools (knowing how to convert letters to numbers and how to reduce numbers to a single digit) to explore these additional personal numbers on your own and gain further insight into your behaviors, illnesses, and personal challenges. Use the Positive and Negative Interpretations of the Numbers, beginning on page 18, for a basic interpretation of these additional numbers. To delve deeper into the qualities of the numbers, you may also want to consult a basic numerology book (see Recommended Reading).

• The first name represents the physical self, your health, finances, professional relationships, and how you behave every day, espe-

1	2	3	4	5	6	7	8	9
A	B	C	D	E	F	G	H	I
J	K	L	M	N	O	P	Q	R
S	T	U	V	W	X	Y	Z

Finding Your Challenge Numbers **43**

cially at work. Working consciously with this energy can open the doorway to your soul's purpose for being here (the vowel total; see below).

- The middle name represents the emotional self, how you behave in relationships, and what you seek in a partner. If someone does not have a middle name, he is here to work on balancing and expressing his emotions. In some cultures, middle names are not used and the general population can be either emotionally intense or emotionally flat.

- The last name represents your relationship with your birth or adopted family, the lessons you are to learn from them and they from you. It's also a number that can guide you in a spiritual direction.

- The sum of the vowels in your full birth name represents your soul's purpose for being here, validation of the contract you signed with the God energy.

- The sum of the consonants in your full birth name represents your personality's physical, emotional, and mental aspects.

- The total of all of the letters in a name represents "the face the world sees" and the type of work preferred.

- Your month, day, and year of birth identify your destiny, determine your life challenges and soulutions, your mental approach to life (subcycles), and the timing of physical events (pinnacles).

- By adding the sum total of a name to the sum total of the month/day/year of birth, the life calling can be identified. Working with this energy allows one to make a quantum leap forward in soul evolution and fulfill childhood dreams.

4

Identifying the Soulutions
to Your Challenges

Using the achievement number, you can identify the inherent challenge and accompanying soulution for any personal number. In this book, personal numbers (sometimes called prime numbers) are determined through your name and birth date and include the achievement number, minor and major life challenges, and karmic lessons. The numbers associated with any illnesses or diseases you have are also personal numbers. Using the numeric analysis of your health condition (given in chapter 5) and the following challenge/soulution chart that corresponds to your achievement number, you can identify the challenges associated with your health issues and the soulutions that will bring healing.

If you wish to extend this practice further, a personal number could really come from anything in your life that can be converted to a number. You could add together the digits of a phone number or address to analyze their numeric energies. You could convert the names of emotions, dreams, cravings, impulsive behaviors, foods, businesses, countries, or ideas to numbers in order to discover the associated challenges and soulutions. Before you begin, let's look at a quick example. If your achievement number is 1 and you want to discover the challenges and soulutions of the number 5 (perhaps because it is your major challenge number or because you had tonsillitis, which is numerically associated with the number 5), you would locate the 5 on the first chart below and find the challenge (9) and soulution (8) numbers on the lines underneath. You would record these numbers by writing the number 5 followed by the fraction 9/8 (5 9/8). The top number of the fraction is always the challenge number and the bottom number is always the soulution.

Achievement Number 1

Personal Number	1 2 3 4 **5** 6 7 8 9
Challenge	1 3 5 7 **9** 2 4 6 8
Soulution	9 2 4 6 **8** 1 3 5 7

Achievement Number 2

Personal Number	1 2 3 4 5 6 7 8 9
Challenge	9 2 4 6 8 1 3 5 7
Soulution	7 9 2 4 6 8 1 3 5

Achievement Number 3

Personal Number	1 2 3 4 5 6 7 8 9
Challenge	8 1 3 5 7 9 2 4 6
Soulution	5 7 9 2 4 6 8 1 3

Achievement Number 4

Personal Number	1 2 3 4 5 6 7 8 9
Challenge	7 9 2 4 6 8 1 3 5
Soulution	3 5 7 9 2 4 6 8 1

Achievement Number 5

Personal Number	1 2 3 4 5 6 7 8 9
Challenge	6 8 1 3 5 7 9 2 4
Soulution	1 3 5 7 9 2 4 6 8

Achievement Number 6

Personal Number	1 2 3 4 5 6 7 8 9
Challenge	5 7 9 2 4 6 8 1 3
Soulution	8 1 3 5 7 9 2 4 6

Achievement Number 7

Personal Number	1 2 3 4 5 6 7 8 9
Challenge	4 6 8 1 3 5 7 9 2
Soulution	6 8 1 3 5 7 9 2 4

Achievement Number 8

Personal Number	1 2 3 4 5 6 7 8 9
Challenge	3 5 7 9 2 4 6 8 1
Soulution	4 6 8 1 3 5 7 9 2

Achievement Number 9

Personal Number	1 2 3 4 5 6 7 8 9
Challenge	2 4 6 8 1 3 5 7 9
Soulution	2 4 6 8 1 3 5 7 9

The negative interpretations of the numbers are used when analyzing a challenge or illness. The positive aspects of a number are the soulution, the key to healing. Identifying the specific soulutions for each challenge allows us to consciously change our behavior patterns to begin the healing process.

The negative patterns that present themselves as challenges and increase negative energy in the body along with the positive soulutions that are the key to healing are presented here:

1 • Issues of the Ego Self

> **Challenge:** Ego too strong or too weak, arrogant, timid, not centered, low self-esteem, stubborn, egotistical, may be a bully
>
> *Soulution:* Get centered, develop confidence, and become a leader

2 • Issues Involving Communication and Interaction with Others

Challenge: Codependent, uncooperative, issues with sensitivity and emotions (too much or too little), may be too blunt

Soulution: Speak up, express feelings and emotions, let go of emotional and sentimental attachments, and practice harmony

3 • Issues Involving Social Interactions and Acceptance of Self and Others

Challenge: Feelings of inadequacy, boastful, exaggeration, scattered, unforgiving, sarcastic, moody, a gossip

Soulution: Become proficient at something (be it creating Jell-O molds or playing golf), be more creative, be confident, and finish things

4 • Issues Involving "Getting It Done": Procrastination, Control, and Constrictions

Challenge: Procrastination, controlling, stubborn, dull, stern, mean, narrow-minded, judgmental

Soulution: Use system, order, and structure to make things happen

5 • Issues Involving Change and Movement

Challenge: Rigid, careless, impulsive, yields too quickly, does to excess (be it food, sex, or work)

Soulution: Learn to be flexible, allow change, and have the confidence to be in the moment

6 • Issues Involving Responsibility to Family, Community, and Relationships

Challenge: Perfectionist or irresponsible, martyr, interfering, nagging, difficulty with emotional intimacy, tends to have unrealistic expectations of self and/or others

Soulution: Make yourself your first priority

7 • Issues Involving Trust, Skepticism, and Control

Challenge: Overly analytical/logical, impatient, controlling, anxious, lacks faith in positive outcome (full of doubt), skeptical, and deceitful

Soulution: Learn to trust—yourself, then Spirit, then others

8 • Issues Involving Power, Money, Control, and Status

Challenge: Anger, tendency to bully and be rebellious, materialistic, confrontational, easily frustrated, abuses power, seeks power for control

Soulution: Walk your talk. Become a leader and use your natural abilities to organize, orchestrate, and delegate to accomplish tasks and goals

9 • Issues Involving Selflessness

Challenge: Egotistical, controlling, needy, carries burdens for others (martyr), has difficulty expressing emotions or asking for help

Soulution: Release the past and embrace the future, and learn to serve with love

DAISY CHAINS: ANALYZING YOUR NUMBER PATTERNS

The daisy chain process I have created takes any personal number and, by following a chain of challenges and soulutions associated with that number, generates a string of digits that reveals personal healing patterns. This simple process is one of the most powerful tools available to assist you in healing.

Numeric daisy chains are similar to flower chains in which flowers are linked together until they complete a circle, with the last flower linking with the first. The numeric daisy chains reveal the types of experiences that can be catalysts for changing nonproductive and stress-producing behavior patterns. The first number of the numeric

```
1 2 3 4 5 6 7 8 9
A B C D E F G H I
J K L M N O P Q R
S T U V W X Y Z
```
Identifying the Soulutions to Your Challenges   **49**

daisy chain is determined by selecting any of your personal numbers—a challenge number or the number that represents a personal health issue. The chain then follows a challenge/soulution sequence until the initial number selected reappears as the final soulution number. Here is a visual example of a numeric daisy chain using a 6 achievement number and the personal number 4 to determine the challenge/soulution sequence. (The regular-size numbers are soulutions and the superscripted numbers are the challenges): $4\,{}^2\,5\,{}^4\,7\,{}^8\,2\,{}^7\,1\,{}^5\,8\,{}^1\,4$

The chains give us the insight necessary to turn our life choices from reactive to proactive. It's very difficult to break lifelong patterns but it's even more difficult to recognize them. Numeric daisy chains can identify the cause-and-effect relationships among behavior patterns, life choices, illnesses, diseases, and physical injuries. They reveal hidden behavioral influences beneath the surface of our outer selves.

Imagine you're at a carnival and decide to have your picture taken standing behind one of those full-size, costumed cardboard or plywood cutouts. You stand behind the cutout with only your face showing through and have your picture taken. When the picture is developed, only the outer self is visible; this is the facade, the picture that the world sees. Sometimes, it's also as much as we want to know about ourselves. The daisy chains reveal hidden aspects that are important to understanding who we are and why we behave or react the way we do.

FINDING YOUR DAISY CHAINS

To determine your daisy chains, you can use the **Challenge**/*Soulution* chart corresponding to your achievement number (beginning on page 45). Proficiency in using this chart will help you identify the events to be experienced and the lessons to be learned while moving from point A to point B on your life's journey.

Begin by selecting a personal number—it could be the total for an illness or disease; the achievement number; life challenges; karmic lessons; the total of your first, middle, or last name; or any other major number in your life.

Once you select a number, find its challenge and soulution and then use the soulution number as your next personal number. Follow the chain of challenges and soulutions until the original number reappears as a soulution.

While it can be an extremely valuable process to find your own numeric chains, I have also provided all eighty-one numeric daisy chains of the human personality matrix (nine chains for each of the nine achievement numbers) here for convenience and to allow us to look at some of the larger patterns within the chains.

Remember, full-size numbers are soulutions and the superscripted numbers are challenges.

Achievement Number 1

$1^1 9^8 7^4 3^5 4^7 6^2 1$
$2^3 2$
$3^5 4^7 6^2 1^1 9^8 7^4 3$
$4^7 6^2 1^1 9^8 7^4 3^5 4$
$5^9 8^6 5$
$6^2 1^1 9^8 7^4 3^5 4^7 6$
$7^4 3^5 4^7 6^2 1^1 9^8 7$
$8^6 5^9 8$
$9^8 7^4 3^5 4^7 6^2 1^1 9$

Achievement Number 2

$1^9 7^3 1$
$2^2 9^7 5^8 6^1 8^5 3^4 2$
$3^4 2^2 9^7 5^8 6^1 8^5 3$
$4^6 4$
$5^8 6^1 8^5 3^4 2^2 9^7 5$
$6^1 8^5 3^4 2^2 9^7 5^8 6$
$7^3 1^9 7$
$8^5 3^4 2^2 9^7 5^8 6^1 8$
$9^7 5^8 6^1 8^5 3^4 2^2 9$

Achievement Number 3

$1^8 5^7 4^5 2^1 7^2 8^4 1$
$2^1 7^2 8^4 1^8 5^7 4^5 2$
$3^3 9^6 3$
$4^5 2^1 7^2 8^4 1^8 5^7 4$
$5^7 4^5 2^1 7^2 8^4 1^8 5$
$6^9 6$
$7^2 8^4 1^8 5^7 4^5 2^1 7$
$8^4 1^8 5^7 4^5 2^1 7^2 8$
$9^6 3^3 9$

Achievement Number 4

$1^7 3^2 7^1 6^8 4^4 9^5 1$
$2^9 5^6 2$
$3^2 7^1 6^8 4^4 9^5 1^7 3$
$4^4 9^5 1^7 3^2 7^1 6^8 4$
$5^6 2^9 5$
$6^8 4^4 9^5 1^7 3^2 7^1 6$
$7^1 6^8 4^4 9^5 1^7 3^2 7$
$8^3 8$
$9^5 1^7 3^2 7^1 6^8 4^4 9$

Achievement Number 5

$1\,^6\,1$

$2\,^8\,3\,^1\,5\,^5\,9\,^4\,8\,^2\,6\,^7\,2$

$3\,^1\,5\,^5\,9\,^4\,8\,^2\,6\,^7\,2\,^8\,3$

$4\,^3\,7\,^9\,4$

$5\,^5\,9\,^4\,8\,^2\,6\,^7\,2\,^8\,3\,^1\,5$

$6\,^7\,2\,^8\,3\,^1\,5\,^5\,9\,^4\,8\,^2\,6$

$7\,^9\,4\,^3\,7$

$8\,^2\,6\,^7\,2\,^8\,3\,^1\,5\,^5\,9\,^4\,8$

$9\,^4\,8\,^2\,6\,^7\,2\,^8\,3\,^1\,5\,^5\,9$

Achievement Number 6

$1\,^5\,8\,^1\,4\,^2\,5\,^4\,7\,^8\,2\,^7\,1$

$2\,^7\,1\,^5\,8\,^1\,4\,^2\,5\,^4\,7\,^8\,2$

$3\,^9\,3$

$4\,^2\,5\,^4\,7\,^8\,2\,^7\,1\,^5\,8\,^1\,4$

$5\,^4\,7\,^8\,2\,^7\,1\,^5\,8\,^1\,4\,^2\,5$

$6\,^6\,9\,^3\,6$

$7\,^8\,2\,^7\,1\,^5\,8\,^1\,4\,^2\,5\,^4\,7$

$8\,^1\,4\,^2\,5\,^4\,7\,^8\,2\,^7\,1\,^5\,8$

$9\,^3\,6\,^6\,9$

Achievement Number 7

$1\,^4\,6\,^5\,7\,^7\,9\,^2\,4\,^1\,3\,^8\,1$

$2\,^6\,8\,^9\,2$

$3\,^8\,1\,^4\,6\,^5\,7\,^7\,9\,^2\,4\,^1\,3$

$4\,^1\,3\,^8\,1\,^4\,6\,^5\,7\,^7\,9\,^2\,4$

$5\,^3\,5$

$6\,^5\,7\,^7\,9\,^2\,4\,^1\,3\,^8\,1\,^4\,6$

$7\,^7\,9\,^2\,4\,^1\,3\,^8\,1\,^4\,6\,^5\,7$

$8\,^9\,2\,^6\,8$

$9\,^2\,4\,^1\,3\,^8\,1\,^4\,6\,^5\,7\,^7\,9$

Achievement Number 8

$1\,^3\,4\,^9\,1$

$2\,^5\,6\,^4\,5\,^2\,3\,^7\,8\,^8\,9\,^1\,2$

$3\,^7\,8\,^8\,9\,^1\,2\,^5\,6\,^4\,5\,^2\,3$

$4\,^9\,1\,^3\,4$

$5\,^2\,3\,^7\,8\,^8\,9\,^1\,2\,^5\,6\,^4\,5$

$6\,^4\,5\,^2\,3\,^7\,8\,^8\,9\,^1\,2\,^5\,6$

$7\,^6\,7$

$8\,^8\,9\,^1\,2\,^5\,6\,^4\,5\,^2\,3\,^7\,8$

$9\,^1\,2\,^5\,6\,^4\,5\,^2\,3\,^7\,8\,^8\,9$

Achievement Number 9

$1\,^2\,2\,^4\,4\,^8\,8\,^7\,7\,^5\,5\,^1\,1$

$2\,^4\,4\,^8\,8\,^7\,7\,^5\,5\,^1\,1\,^2\,2$

$3\,^6\,6\,^3\,3$

$4\,^8\,8\,^7\,7\,^5\,5\,^1\,1\,^2\,2\,^4\,4$

$5\,^1\,1\,^2\,2\,^4\,4\,^8\,8\,^7\,7\,^5\,5$

$6\,^3\,3\,^6\,6$

$7\,^5\,5\,^1\,1\,^2\,2\,^4\,4\,^8\,8\,^7\,7$

$8\,^7\,7\,^5\,5\,^1\,1\,^2\,2\,^4\,4\,^8\,8$

$9\,^9\,9$

INTERPRETING THE DAISY CHAINS

To decipher the soulution (positive) and challenge (negative) numbers of your numeric daisy chains, use both the Positive and Negative Interpretations of the Numbers in chapter 2 (beginning on page 18) and the **Challenge**/*Soulution* descriptions, which begin on page 46.

The positive interpretations of the soulutions tell us the positive behavior patterns that, if practiced in daily life, enable us to make pro-active life decisions rather than reactive choices. The negative interpretations of the challenges are the patterns that must be recognized and overcome.

In this section we will look at three examples of how to interpret and use daisy chains. We will begin with an example of how to interpret daisy chains related to an illness. (Again, the illnesses themselves will be presented and interpreted in chapter 5.) This is followed by examples of how to analyze daisy chains associated with work and relationship patterns. We will conclude by looking at the significance of the length of the daisy chains and recurring patterns within the chains.

Note that in the interpretation examples, the numbers given in parentheses embody the qualities being discussed.

EXAMPLE: USING DAISY CHAINS TO UNDERSTAND THE CATALYSTS FOR BREAST CANCER

In this example I have chosen to analyze the challenges and soulutions associated with the behavior patterns that are catalysts for breast cancer for someone with an achievement number of 6.

The 6 achievement number is characterized by a tendency to take on too much responsibility for others' happiness and to have unrealistic expectations. (See the complete description of this achievement number on page 27.) Those who have a 2, 6, 7, or 9 as their achievement number may be more prone to developing breast cancer because of a tendency toward codependency. The numbers for breast cancer are

46/1, indicating an oversensitivity to the needs of others. Individuals with breast cancer may feel that they need to be the foundation others can rely on, which causes a suppression of the self (1) for the sake of a relationship (6). (See the complete Breast Cancer interpretation on page 82.)

To analyze the numeric patterns associated with breast cancer (for someone with a 6 achievement number), we will look at the daisy chains, the challenge and soulution paths, of the numbers for breast cancer: 4, 6, and 1. The three daisy chains are as follows:

$$4^2 5^4 7^8 2^7 1^5 8^1 4$$
$$6^6 9^3 6$$
$$1^5 8^1 4^2 5^4 7^8 2^7 1$$

A Note on Daisy Chaining Illnesses

If an illness or disease is composed of several digits, daisy chain each digit. For example, the numbers for breast cancer are 46/1. Examine the 4, 6, and 1. This gives deeper insight into the behavior patterns that are the catalysts for the disease and helps explain why this "1" responds the way it does.

First I'll explain the negative behavior patterns associated with the superscripted challenge numbers. Then I'll explain how following the path of the positive soulution numbers can help change the overall behavior pattern and bring about a change in the energetic frequencies of breast cancer.

$$4^2 5^4 7^8 2^7 1^5 8^1 4$$

Interpretation of challenge numbers 2, 4, 8, 7, 5, 1: Oversensitivity to the needs of others (2) leads to a need to be in control (4), which brings

54 Identifying the Soulutions to Your Challenges

1	2	3	4	5	6	7	8	9
A	B	C	D	E	F	G	H	I
J	K	L	M	N	O	P	Q	R
S	T	U	V	W	X	Y	Z	

frustration and loss of personal empowerment (8), impatience, fear of not being good enough and disappointing others, or concerns related to abandonment issues (7). This leads to extremes of rigidity or flexibility (5) in an effort to please others, which results in a lowering of self-esteem (1).

Interpretation of soulution numbers 4, 5, 7, 2, 1, 8, 4: Creating a solid personal foundation (4) that is flexible (5) is key to comprehending (7) the "big picture" and allowing/encouraging others to take more personal responsibility for their actions and choices (2). Developing the courage to do what is loved (1) brings self-empowerment, recognition, and success (8). To accomplish this, these individuals must use the power, wisdom, and knowledge gained through lifetimes to organize, orchestrate, and delegate to others (8). This makes them the architect of their life and the lives of those around them (4). There is a huge difference between being an architect who designs plans and delegates to others to carry them out and the martyrs who attempt to do everything themselves . . . hoping to be appreciated for their efforts and sacrifices.

$6^6 9^3 6$

Interpretation of challenge numbers 6 and 3: Unrealistic expectations for self and others (6) can manifest feelings of inadequacy (3), which may lead individuals to resent those they were trying to help (3). The 3 can also indicate a tendency to scatter personal energy by trying to do too much for too many, with too little.

Interpretation of soulution numbers 6, 9, 6: The first 6 calls for individuals to be mentors, counselors, or advisers—not *clingers, enablers, doers,* or *controllers.* They must learn to guide people to their own revelations via the Socratic method of questioning, asking nonjudgmental questions *and waiting* for the answers. Allowing others to "own" their conclusions will lead them to thank these individuals rather than telling them to butt out! The positive 9 requires doing things out of love, not because it will lead to being loved. The 9 also calls for letting go of emotional attachments to outcomes. The final 6 brings opportunities to practice emotional intimacy on every level of every relationship—whether with family, in intimate relationships, with friends or coworkers. Emotional intimacy is having the courage to speak truth with love and not being influenced by what others think or do. This 6 also calls for compassion, empathy, and service to others.

$1^5 8^1 4^2 5^4 7^8 2^7 1$

The final chain is initiated by the personal number 1, which represents the other two numbers (the 4 and 6 of 46) combined and distilled to a core issue (4 + 6 = 10, which reduces to 1). In this instance, the 1 represents a lack of confidence, a weak identity that is based on feedback from others, not making the self the first priority, and accepting responsibility for less-than-desirable outcomes.

Interpretation of challenge numbers 5, 1, 2, 4, 8, 7: The challenge numbers can be interpreted in two different ways. Individuals may be overly amenable (5); have low self-esteem (1); be overly sensitive to the inputs or needs of others (2); get lost in details, resist change, or have a need to control outcomes (4); suffer with frustration, hidden anger, and/or an inability to step into power (8). The final number in the chain, 7, can bring fears of abandonment, humiliation, ostracism, and trust (whether it's of themselves, others, or Spirit). In the alternative interpretation, rigidity (5); arrogance (1); insensitivity (2); a tendency to be controlling (4), domineering, angry (8), and a "know it all" (7) leads individuals to believe that they are entitled to voice their opinion, whether or not you want it (7).

Interpretation of soulution numbers 1, 8, 4, 5, 7, 2, 1: Individuals must honor themselves by doing what feels right in their heart (1); stepping into power and leading others by "walking the talk" (8); and not procrastinating or waiting for preapproval of ideas before making them a reality (4). Individuals must learn to accept the moment as all there is and to accept change (5). They must acknowledge that Spirit knows more than they do and that there is a divine plan that they themselves

56   Identifying the Soulutions to Your Challenges

```
1 2 3 4 5 6 7 8 9
A B C D E F G H I
J K L M N O P Q R
S T U V W X Y Z
```

helped cocreate (7). Via tact, diplomacy, and good communication skills, these individuals must become the arbitrators, mediators, and facilitators in their interactions with others (2); and become centered and self-accepting and initiate and lead by example (1).

EXAMPLE: USING DAISY CHAINS TO UNDERSTAND WORK PATTERNS

The first name is associated with work patterns. In this example we will analyze the daisy chain for a woman with the first name Lynn and an 8 achievement number. The name Lynn transposes to a number 2 and yields the following daisy chain: $2\ ^5\ 6\ ^4\ 5\ ^2\ 3\ ^7\ 8\ ^8\ 9\ ^1\ 2$.

The daisy chain tells us that to become a positive 2—a harmonizer, mediator, diplomat, and balancer—Lynn must learn to communicate, trust her intuition, and let go of emotional and sentimental attachments by becoming more flexible and confident and less rigid (5 challenge). She must be of service (6 soulution), not procrastinate or be stubborn (4 challenge), and remain flexible and moderate in all actions (5 soulution). Lynn must learn to overcome timidity or an uncooperative nature (2 challenge) to cooperate and communicate. She must learn self-acceptance (3 soulution) and be more creative and tolerant by letting go of fear (7 challenge). This can be done by acquiring knowledge; confidence; and the ability to initiate, orchestrate, and delegate (8 soulution). These skills will eliminate frustration (8 challenge) by relinquishing the ego's need for recognition, appreciation, and thanks for doing the "right" thing (9 soulution). Egocentric patterns (1 challenge) will also be eliminated, leading to a more cooperative (2 soulution) and flexible attitude toward being of service to others.

EXAMPLE: USING DAISY CHAINS TO UNDERSTAND RELATIONSHIP PATTERNS

The middle name represents the emotional self and indicates how we behave in relationships. For this example we will analyze a person with

```
1 2 3 4 5 6 7 8 9
A B C D E F G H I
J K L M N O P Q R
S T U V W X Y Z
```
Identifying the Soulutions to Your Challenges **57**

the middle name Richard (which transposes to a 7) and an 8 achievement number. With a middle-name number of 7, this individual has control and abandonment issues and finds it easier to give than receive. With the emotional self under the influence of the 7, he may be a great lover or may be cold and emotionally distant. The main issue is learning to trust and open up to another by becoming more vulnerable.

This combination yields a very short daisy chain of only three numbers: 7 ⁶ 7. The 6 challenge indicates that this is someone who may get involved with people with "broken wings" (individuals with "potential" that never materializes). He wants to fix people and, thereby, be validated for his wisdom and knowledge. Being validated counters abandonment feelings. The 6 challenge also brings forth a tendency toward perfectionism as well as unrealistic emotional expectations for the self and others. There can be a tinge of martyrdom. The 7 soulution says that for this individual to experience satisfactory relationships, he must overcome anxieties associated with betrayal and abandonment, let go of control, and stop trying to fix everyone and everything. He must allow himself to become vulnerable.

DAISY CHAIN LENGTH

The shortest daisy chain has three digits and the longest chain has thirteen. The length of a numeric string is determined by how soon the original number is regenerated as the soulution.

It is not an accident that the shortest chain is three digits long. Symbolically, 3 can be associated with focusing on a specific behavior, idea, or intention. The positive number 3 represents the power to create, to give birth to dreams and visions, and to be emotionally intimate (speaking one's truth from the heart). The extreme negative 3 has such feelings of inadequacy that she withdraws deep into a cave to avoid social interactions or can be very sarcastic and unforgiving, producing huge amounts of stress in the mental, emotional, and physical bodies.

The three-digit daisy chain offers either a quick soulution or

58 Identifying the Soulutions to Your Challenges

```
1  2  3  4  5  6  7  8  9
A  B  C  D  E  F  G  H  I
J  K  L  M  N  O  P  Q  R
S  T  U  V  W  X  Y  Z
```

repetitive frustration. The energy of a short daisy chain can be very intense. We consciously create our three-digit daisy chains and direct them to appear at specific times when we are ready to change our life, ready to decode the life plan created with the God energies. By consciously completing the circle created by the daisy chain, we can experience a quantum leap forward in accepting that we are an integral part of the energy of creation.

Examples of the Shortest (Three-Digit) Daisy Chains

The shortest chain for an achievement number of 1 is 2 ^{3} 2: With an achievement number of 1, we know there are issues revolving around self-esteem, whether they are displayed as timidity or arrogance or a combination of the two. With this background, the 3 challenge implies that this individual has difficulty with some or all of the following scenarios involving communication and interaction with others (2). This individual may be unforgiving toward those he feels have let him down. The 2 soulution indicates a need to let go of emotional attachments, speak up in a timely manner, and compromise. If the individual has difficulty following through without encouragement or support from others, the 2 soulution indicates a need to trust his intuition. There is also the possibility of difficulty with social interactions, leading to withdrawal and sarcasm. In this case, the 2 soulution indicates a need to be more tactful, diplomatic, and compromising.

The shortest chain for an achievement number of 5 is 1 ^{6} 1: With an achievement number of 5, this individual has issues with flexibility, confidence, and dealing with transitions. The 6 challenge indicates unrealistic expectations for the self and others. Taking care of others (6) is used as an excuse for not moving forward one's own life (1). Sometimes this is taken to the point of martyrdom. If this individual cannot do things right, according to her standards, she will not do them at all. The 1 soulution is to have the confidence to be true to the self.

The shortest chain for an achievement number of 9 is 9 ^{9} 9: This is the

1	2	3	4	5	6	7	8	9
A	B	C	D	E	F	G	H	I
J	K	L	M	N	O	P	Q	R
S	T	U	V	W	X	Y	Z

Identifying the Soulutions to Your Challenges **59**

most intense of all of the three-digit chains, as it calls for accepting the fact that nothing is forever, except change. The 9 achievement number represents a final exam that includes all of the other challenges (1–9) as part of the 9 challenge. This individual has chosen to learn to let go of all control in this lifetime, as well as to learn to love unconditionally, with no expectations of being loved in return. This particular chain emphasizes learning to do what you love, not to be loved or to maintain control (to ensure that everything works according to his perception of reality).

Example of the Longest (Thirteen-Digit) Daisy Chain
The longest daisy chains are composed of thirteen digits. The number 13 represents opportunities for transition. It is the number for making innovative visions into reality. The 13 calls for recognizing and releasing feelings of low self-esteem (1) and inadequacy (3). The 4 total (1 + 3 = 4) calls for building a new foundation.

Let's take a look at a thirteen-digit daisy chain for the 1 achievement number. With an achievement number of 1, the core issues are to overcome passivity or aggressiveness, egocentricity, low self-esteem, fearfulness, being a zealot, timidity, being a bully, arrogance, and having no sense of self. The negative 1 needs to become a positive 1 by becoming self-directed, assertive, energetic, and balanced; by following internal guidance, being an initiator, and being comfortable with self; by being a leader, paradigm-buster, and innovator; by being proactive rather than reactive to life's situations.

The 7 ^{4}3 ^{5}4 ^{7}6 ^{2}1 ^{1}9 ^{8}7 daisy chain tells an individual to learn to trust, be more intuitive and patient, and allow the universe to be his guide (7 soulution). This individual should avoid trying to control life; stop procrastinating or being overly logical (4 challenge); become more optimistic, focused, and a better communicator (3 soulution); avoid impulsiveness, rigidity, or excess flexibility (5 challenge); pay attention to details, complete what he starts, and build a solid foundation (4 soulution). He must release the need to be needed as well as concerns about

1	2	3	4	5	6	7	8	9
A	B	C	D	E	F	G	H	I
J	K	L	M	N	O	P	Q	R
S	T	U	V	W	X	Y	Z	

being humiliated or belittled for not always having the "right" answer (7 challenge). He must make a conscious effort to become a mentor, not a martyr, and willingly be of service to others (6 soulution). He must recognize codependency issues; release emotional and sentimental attachments (2 challenge); believe in himself and his abilities and gifts (1 soulution); avoid arrogance or timidity (1 challenge); and whatever he does, it must be done from love (9 soulution). He must not become frustrated or angry if things don't happen the way he wants them to, and not be afraid of growing self-empowerment (8 challenge). The last number represents what this individual can become—accepting of the divine plan; patient; a life teacher; a healer; peaceful; in harmony with self, others, and the universe (7 soulution).

PATTERNS WITHIN THE CHAINS

With the daisy chains arranged in vertical lists under the achievement numbers (see page 50), it is easy to see how number patterns are repeated, causing the same patterns of behavior in many aspects of a personality. These overlapping patterns can explain why you behave the way you do in your daily actions and interactions with family, friends, coworkers, partners, and the world at large. Recognizing and acknowledging the most repetitive patterns in your numeric chains will enable you to make more proactive life choices. Acknowledgment and action are the means of reestablishing harmony between yourself and the universe.

Among the sets of nine numeric chains for each achievement number, each has its own set of seven repetitive number patterns. To highlight these patterns, which reoccur throughout the nine numeric chains, I have used a single underline, double underline, bolded numbers, ovals, brackets, and two arrows extending from a dotted line (indicating the 3 ^{3} 9 and 9 ^{6} 3 patterns) in the following example of the 3 achievement number. Notice that there are always two five-digit daisy chains that mirror each other.

Achievement Number 3: Numeric Daisy Chains

$$1\ ^8 5\ ^7 4\ ^5 \left[2\ ^1 7\ ^2 8\ ^4 1\right]$$

$$\left[2\ ^1 7\ ^2 8\ ^4 1\ ^8 5\ ^7 4\ ^5 2\right]$$

$$3\ ^3 9\ ^6 3$$

$$4\ ^5 \left[2\ ^1 7\ ^2 8\ ^4 1\ ^8 5\ ^7 4\right]$$

$$5\ ^7 4\ ^5 \left[2\ ^1 7\ ^2 8\ ^4 1\ ^8 5\right]$$

$$6\ ^9 6$$

$$7\ ^2 8\ ^4 1\ ^8 5\ ^7 4\ ^5 \left[2\ ^1 7\right]$$

$$8\ ^4 1\ ^8 5\ ^7 4\ ^5 \left[2\ ^1 7\ ^2 8\right]$$

$$9\ ^6 3\ ^3 9$$

The two patterns that recur most frequently in this example are portions of the $1\ ^8 5\ ^7 4\ ^5 2\ ^1 7\ ^2 8\ ^4 1$ and $7\ ^2 8\ ^4 1\ ^8 5\ ^7 4\ ^5 2\ ^1 7$ chains. The 1 chain deals with issues involving the ego-self; the 7 chain represents issues revolving around abandonment and control.

The main challenge associated with the 3 achievement number is overcoming feelings of insecurity, inferiority, or inadequacy. The soulution is to master something (anything!) and finish what is started. For a complete description of this achievement number, refer back to page 26.

Keeping in mind the characteristics of the 3 achievement number, read the following interpretation of the $1\ ^8 5\ ^7 4\ ^5 2\ ^1 7\ ^2 8\ ^4 1$ numeric chain to see the actions this individual is to avoid as well as those she is to follow to embody the positive 1: To be a confident leader (1 soulution), this individual must overcome the frustration that no one is listening as well as the fear of success (8 challenges). She must step into her

1	2	3	4	5	6	7	8	9
A	B	C	D	E	F	G	H	I
J	K	L	M	N	O	P	Q	R
S	T	U	V	W	X	Y	Z	

62   Identifying the Soulutions to Your Challenges

power by having the confidence to be in the moment (5 soulution) and let go of the need to "figure out everything" in advance in an attempt to avoid potential humiliation or embarrassment (7 challenge). Building a more solid foundation by slowing down, paying more attention to details (4 soulution), becoming more flexible and learning to be in the moment (5 challenge), this individual begins to realize that the more she trusts her inner feelings, the more harmony appears in her life (2 soulution). She can overcome self-esteem issues (1 challenge) by realizing that she has always been divinely supported (7 soulution). Codependency issues are the next to be released (2 challenge). The 8 soulution indicates leadership opportunities for using the wisdom, knowledge, and expertise gained through many lifetimes. The 8 is also about having the confidence to "walk the talk." There is no longer a need to be in control (4 challenge). The final soulution of 1 results in this individual melding her divine self with her physical self, having the courage to break existing paradigms and break through the tangled web of abandonment issues into the clearing of who she is and why she is here.

Look for the seven repetitive numeric patterns in your own nine daisy chains; then find the two most repetitive patterns and focus on changing them. When you begin living these two patterns proactively, by choosing to live the soulutions and address the challenges, you will restore harmony to your life.

Used regularly and consistently, the practice of analyzing the daisy chains can illuminate the reasons why we behave the way we do at home, in relationships, and at work, enabling us to have the wisdom, knowledge, and courage to make ourself our first priority. Making this choice shifts us from a container that can be drained (clinger, enabler, doer, or controller) to a perpetual spring.

I cannot stress enough the importance of learning and understanding the positive and negative characteristics for each number. It may be a bit daunting at first, like learning a new language, but it is well worth the effort. The more proficiency you gain with the numbers, the more personal insights and revelations are experienced.

Like a sunrise bringing light to a dark world, your proficiency in understanding your numeric daisy chains can shed more light on the causes of your health issues and other negative aspects of your life. You will most likely want to return to this chapter after reading the interpretations of your health concerns in the following chapter for insights on interpreting your daisy chains, the personal numeric patterns, associated with the illness in question.

5

Numeric Interpretations
of Specific Illnesses
and Diseases

For each illness or disease analyzed in this chapter, the letters of the condition's name are transposed to a numeric sum, which is provided parenthetically in the disease heading. (If you need a reminder of how these sums are figured, refer back to the explanation in chapter 2.) In the interpretations, the numbers given in parentheses either embody the particular qualities being discussed or are the numeric total of the given word or phrase. Sometimes I provide analysis for different names of the same condition. For instance, we can gain greater insight by analyzing both acquired immune deficiency syndrome and AIDS, which have different numeric totals. With many of the conditions listed in this chapter, it will be fairly obvious how I have arrived at the interpretations. With others, where it was necessary to go into greater depth with the analysis in order to get to the essence of the problem or to explore all of the nuances, it may be less clear. Don't worry about figuring it all out. Read the interpretations and see how the patterns described relate to your own life or to those whom you are trying to understand or to assist in their own healing journeys. Reflect on the relevance of the positive and negative qualities of the numbers, analyze the relationship between the disease numbers and your personal numbers, and interpret the numeric patterns of challenges and soulutions by using the information provided in the previous chapter.

Before we delve into the interpretations of specific illnesses and diseases, I would like to take a quick look at several key terms that may apply to your various health conditions. The numeric analysis of these terms may provide additional insight into the associated patterns of sickness and the healing soulutions. The terms are placed in order of a general progression from an initial inflammation through acute and chronic conditions and ending with karma, which comes into play when we are unable to complete our lessons in a given lifetime.

Inflammation (55/1): Inflammation is the initial (1) visual manifestation of excess negative energy, the point from which negative energy expands. It is initiated by an internalization of anger or frustration (by the ego) that inhibits forward movement (5).

Pain (22/4): With pain, the physical body—the foundation (4)—seeks attention. Pain is a call to look at foundational issues. Its appearance can be caused by an imbalance in energies relating to sensitivity.

Acute (14/5): An acute episode is the result of a spike of excess negative energy, which causes a physical response of feeling pain. Banging a sore finger on the edge of a table results in acute pain. An acute condition could also take the form of a toothache or stress headache in which there is a sudden constriction (4) in the flow of energy due to low self-esteem (1), lack of self-awareness, or repression of energy.

Infection (50/5): Infection is the movement or spreading of negative energy into adjoining areas. An infection calls attention to what has been ignored. It calls for attentiveness and being present (5) in the moment. It also calls for self-confidence and being able to "let go" and move on.

Chronic (43/7): Control issues, combined with pessimism, make it difficult for the mind/body to heal itself. (Control issues are associated with the universal core issue of abandonment.) Pessimism (3) and procrastination or stubbornness (4) can lead to a long-term depressive state or a state of mental, emotional, or physical paralysis (7).

Illness (27/9): Illness (27/9) is the emotional manifestation of negative energy. The stuffing or internalizing of emotions becomes the catalyst for the physical manifestation of disease (26/8; see below). The numbers for illness represent difficulty with self-expression and the communication of feelings (2), trust, vulnerability, patience, and letting go of a "need to be needed" (7). The 9 indicates a tendency to internalize not only personal emotions but also those of others. The negative 9 can also represent a strong need to be thanked, recognized, appreciated, or loved or the need to control everything.

Disease (26/8): Disease is the manifestation of negative energy in physical form. It involves issues of sensitivity, communication (2), responsibility (6), and personal power (8). Disease is also tied in with karmic lessons that foster change.

Karma (17/8): Fears of abandonment and/or loss of control may prevent an individual from finishing what he started. Karma is unfinished business. The 17/8 represents self-tests (1); learning about trust, vulnerability, patience (7); and issues involving the use or abuse of personal power (8).

Virus (26/8): Viruses are agents for change; they deal with issues of group sensitivity (2), personal responsibility (6), and individual consequences (8). Whether electronic or organic, viruses always affect groups. The appearance of a virus is a direct result of poor communication and shirking personal responsibility. As an agent for change, one of the functions performed by the virus is to strengthen an organism by terminating those life-forms that cannot change.

And now we move on to the glossary of numeric interpretations of illnesses and diseases. As you read the interpretations, notice the number of conditions associated with low self-esteem, poor communication, feelings of inadequacy, control, flexibility, perfectionism, trust, personal empowerment, and a need to be loved. These patterns are all linked to fears of abandonment. The stronger one's feeling of abandonment, the greater the probability of contracting an illness, disease, or physical injury.

> # A
>
> Illnesses and diseases beginning with the letter A have issues of self-esteem as one of the basic causes.

Abscess (14/5)

Inflammation (1), pain (4), and infection (5) are calling attention to the physical (5) body. An abscess represents a refusal to release or verbalize emotions or feelings (9), which then begin to fester and become poisonous.

Acid (17/8) Reflux (32/5) = (49/13/4) / Heartburn (44/8)

Rising from the area of the third chakra, the underlying issue is about personal power (8) and how to express it to others (3 and 2). Situations arise that call for making decisions about one's daily life (44) and the direction in which it is going (5). Acid reflux is anger held back and/or frustration (8) not expressed (3) to others (2). Alternatively, the anger and frustration may spew forth in a tirade (2).

The *burn* of heartburn is a 19/1 indicating that when things are going well, these individuals can be as kind as Mother Teresa (9). However, when things aren't going well, they can become more like

Genghis Khan (1). The 19/1 can also indicate that some emotional pain and suffering is being suppressed. *Heart,* itself, is a 7, indicating a tendency to keep the heart closed for defensive reasons. The 7 also relates to people who don't want to "burden others" with their problems; this is ultimately an abandonment issue and one of self-esteem (1).

The 49/13/4 acid reflux combination indicates control issues (with 4s on either end of the equation) and an inability to let go and transition (13). The 9 is about emotional issues related to being loved or maintaining control and echoes the 7's abandonment issues. The reflux action is the body's way of physically (5) forcing the 8 issues (issues of finance, power, anger, frustration, recognition, status, and rebelliousness) to the surface.

Acne (14/5)

Acne in adolescents (usually occurring on the face, neck, or arms) can indicate a tendency to try to hold back life. By constricting their energy or trying to hold on to the moment, as well as emotions and feelings, adolescents may force these energies in their bodies to find new paths and eventually bubble to the surface. If the individual holds on too tightly, a cyst (13/4—transitions) forms under the surface. (*See also* Cysts.)

Acquired (42/6) Immune (30/3) Deficiency (56/2) Syndrome (41/5) = (169/16/7)

The catalyst for AIDS is a fear of being alone (7). It is about individuals (1) not taking responsibility for their actions (6) because they want love or sex in their life (9). The underlying causes of this behavior pattern are related to abandonment issues (7). The karmic number, 16, indicates the probability of catastrophic events resulting from personal actions that run counter to what you feel is the right thing to do while pushing against the will of the universe.

See also AIDS.

```
1 2 3 4 5 6 7 8 9
A B C D E F G H I
J K L M N O P Q R
S T U V W X Y Z
```
Addiction • Addictions (Narcotics) **69**

Addiction (43/7)

Feelings of inadequacy and poor socialization skills (3), combined with a need to control the environment (4), lead these individuals into a state of mental, emotional, or physical paralysis (7). The 7 total also indicates anxieties associated with abandonment, oversensitivity to the environment, and issues involving vulnerability and control.

Addictions (44/8)

In this instance, the 44/8 indicates a tendency toward confrontation, procrastination, and issues over who's in control (44). There is a pattern of failure to accept personal responsibility or to step into one's personal power (8).

- **Cocaine (32/5):** Sensitivity issues (2) combined with an introvert personality (3) create an artificial extrovert who can swing between impulsiveness and rigidity (5).

- **Crack (15/6):** Uncertain about their place in the physical world (5) and possessing low self-esteem (1) and unrealistic expectations (6), these individuals have difficulty with personal responsibility (6).

- **Heroin (42/6):** The catalysts for addiction are oversensitivity to the environment, weak social and communication skills (all 2 stuff), and a tendency to procrastinate (4) along with a need for community (6) without personal responsibility (6).

- **Narcotics (39/3):** There's difficulty with emotional attachments, especially letting go. These individuals are not "centered"; they are uncertain of who they are. Personality types can be at either extreme—controlling or codependent (9). Under the influence of the negative 3 energy, people always seek to withdraw or keep others at a distance. This is accomplished either by a conscious decision to go within and leave this world or by appearing as an outrageous extrovert but also seeking emotional control. Individuals with a narcotic addiction can be very selfish (33) and see themselves as martyrs. Feelings of emotional inadequacy are also present.

▪ **Nicotine (44/8):** The primary issue is hesitation or procrastination (4 . . . one more puff) in relation to having to make a decision and/or move forward. Core issues involve power, status, money (8), and "getting it done" (4).

▪ **Smoking (34/7):** Control issues (4 and 7) combined with feelings of inadequacy (3) lead to a "smoke screen." Smoking may also be tied in with abandonment issues (7), as well as the need to hold on to something (4) like a security blanket.

▪ **Substance (23/5) Abuse (12/3) = (35/8):** Here there is difficulty dealing with flexibility, moderation, and the physical world (5) due to feelings of inadequacy (3) about self. Poor communication skills (3) lead to anger, frustration, and the misuse of personal power (8).

▪ **Sweets (19/1):** The ego (1) feels it is not receiving enough recognition, appreciation, thanks, or love (9), so the individual seeks more sweetness in life. The 19 always indicates that some form of emotional pain or suffering is present. It also indicates that when things are running smoothly or are pretty much okay, sweets can be controlled. However, if "things" are not okay, the use of sweets can get out of control.
See also Alcoholic *and* Alcoholism.

AIDS (15/6)
The catalyst is self-control issues (1 and 5) in relation to personal responsibility (6). A lack of self-esteem (1) and a tendency toward impulsiveness or a rigid attitude (5) can lead to irresponsible behaviors (6).
See also Acquired Immune Deficiency Syndrome.

Alcoholic (42/6)

An alcoholic has issues revolving around sensitivity and interpersonal communications (2). Also present are issues related to abandonment, control (4), and unrealistic expectations of the self and others (6).

The 42 also indicates a tendency to try to maintain control (4) of one's environment, as others are seen as unreliable or untrustworthy (2). In this state, the individual will try to do it all himself and fail, due to his unrealistic expectations of self and others (6). A common sentiment is "If it can't be done perfectly, why do it at all?" (6).

Alcoholism (44/8)

Those struggling with this disease have an inability to stand up for personal beliefs. Grandiosity and procrastination (44) can lead to internalized and/or externalized anger (8). There are issues involving personal power—either fear of stepping into power or abuse of power.

Allergies (43/7)

These relate to feelings of confidence (3), control (4), and vulnerability (7). Unexpressed feelings or emotions find their way to the surface via the weakest link in the physical body.

Allergy (35/8)

This involves power issues (8) and the need for flexibility, balance, and moderation (5), and issues around communicating (3) feelings to others.

Alzheimer's (53/8) Disease (26/8) = (79/16/7)

First and foremost, this is a disease about learning to let go. The prevalence of 7s indicates codependency issues—needing to be needed. The 8s relate to power and control issues and doing for others grudgingly or not at all. Both numbers indicate being unreceptive to help in any form. Overall there is a strong need to control one's environment. If the individual cannot learn to release the need to be in control,

control is gradually taken from him and he is made dependent on others.

A second consideration as to the cause of Alzheimer's is the need for retaliation. Those for whom this is true have allowed themselves to be controlled by those in their environment, especially by a partner. The manifestation of Alzheimer's can be a passive way of "making" others do for them.

The numeric pattern of 79/16/7 shows that as well as being a result of unresolved issues involving the need to be in control (7), this disease is related to internalizing emotions (9), being overly protective of others (79), having a lack of self-esteem (1), and a concern about making mistakes or being misunderstood (7). I believe that individuals who "contract" this illness have tried to mentally or physically control their environment due to very strong anxieties about being abandoned. They have tried throughout their entire lives to put square pegs into round holes (16). They may see themselves as martyrs (the cause known only to them). They offer advice when it hasn't been asked for and then become frustrated, disappointed, angry, inflexible, or unforgiving when their advice (26/8) or assistance is ignored. Their anxiety (35/8) about not being able to make everything perfect for everyone all of the time (16) places a strain on the nervous system (53/8). They may have a messianic sense of responsibility (16/7)—a need to save or protect everyone and a belief that if they don't, their inadequacies will be pointed out by others (7). There is a tendency to internalize their emotions and not release them (9), placing additional strain on the nervous system. Ultimately, this disease is the catalyst for the soul to complete its lessons about trust, vulnerability, and unconditional love.

Some of the medical catalysts for Alzheimer's disease are listed below. Their numeric equivalents are listed with a brief description of the associated behavior pattern.

■ **Plaques (28/1):** Passive-aggressive pattern (retaliation).

■ **Apolipoprotein (82/1):** Aggressive-passive pattern (control).

■ **Beta Amyloid (42/6):** Sensitivity and communication issues (2) coupled with a desire for control (4) when it comes to involvements with family, community, or work.

Anorexia (42/6) Nervosa (31/4) = (73/10/1)

Oversensitivity (2) and a need for control (4) lead to unrealistic expectations of the self and others (6). A 6 also represents food, family, community, and personal responsibility. Lack of confidence and feelings of inadequacy (3) and anxieties about not being good enough (1) and, therefore, being abandoned (7)—first, by Spirit (10) and then by family (6)—can lead to a desire to hide or withdraw from social contact (3). Ultimately, the individual (1) needs to learn to do what she loves, instead of doing to be loved or to maintain control of an uncontrollable situation.

Anxiety (35/8)

Fear of the physical world (5), feelings of inadequacy (3), and difficulty with personal empowerment can bring on mental, emotional, even physical paralysis. The individual doesn't want to risk making an incorrect decision so she won't move (in any direction). Anxiety is also associated with abandonment issues.

Appendicitis (62/8)

Poor communication (2) within the family unit (6) can lead to repressed anger (8). Hypersensitivity (2) and unrealistic expectations for the self or others (6) breed frustration and anger (8). I believe that one of the purposes of the appendix is to act as an "anger sink"—to be a place where anger is stored. Once the appendix reaches its maximum capacity, it becomes inflamed, then infected, and then bursts.

```
1 2 3 4 5 6 7 8 9
A B C D E F G H I
J K L M N O P Q R
S T U V W X Y Z
```

74 Arteries • Arthritis (Arthritic Fingers)

Arteries (41/5)

Self-esteem issues (1) and constrictive behavior patterns (4), along with a need to be more flexible and moderate (5), can create arterial constrictions and blockages.

Arthritis (50/5)

This disease is associated with flexibility, movement, and interactions with the world (5). We all do things we don't want to do, simply to avoid being abandoned. The longer we do *to* be loved (rigidity) and are not doing *what* we love (flexibility), the greater the probability of manifesting a state of self-imposed immobilization. Arthritis is a subconscious response to an inability to say "No!" The letters *arthr* equal 29/11/2. The 29 indicates a tendency to absorb the emotions of others. The 11, the first master number, brings a hypersensitivity and compulsion to do for others—and feelings of guilt if there is resentment for having to do it. Not wanting to offend others (or be abandoned) by refusing requests, an excuse is sought and found: "I'd love to help but my arthritis is acting up."

Arthritic (52/7) Fingers (42/6) = (94/13/4): The numbers for *arthritic* indicate someone who is overly sensitive (2) and impulsively (5) commits himself to be of service to others (7). Individuals do this not from love, but to be loved and out of fear of abandonment. The arthritis gives them an excuse to limit their activities and service to others without actually having to say no.

Arthritic fingers are the body's reaction to an inability to let go and transition. They are a form of self-paralysis; hands and feet are frozen on the ladder rungs of life. Feelings of low self-esteem and inadequacy (13) make one fearful of reaching out and grabbing life (4). The 9 of the 94 shows a need to be loved, thanked, recognized, or appreciated for "good" deeds. The 4 in this position can indicate a tendency to ignore the self and try to make others the first priority.

▪ **Arthritic (52/7) Joints (24/6) = (76/13/4):** Overconcern for the welfare of others, along with unrealistic expectations of self or others (6), is a major catalyst for arthritic joints. One gives up his or her life (13) and seeks control by taking on unwanted responsibilities (6). There is a stubbornness (4) present about the way life should be. Here, too, arthritic joints (13/4) are the body's reaction to an inability to let go and transition (13). It is a form of self-paralysis; hands and feet are frozen on the ladder rungs of life. Feelings of inadequacy and low self-esteem (13) make one fearful of reaching out—for anything. These individuals feel that if they can make others happy, then everything will be okay. The reality is that we can't make others happy. Happiness is generated internally.

▪ **Rheumatoid (51/6) Arthritis (50) = (101/2):** Here is another example of physically putting others (2) before self (1). There is also a tendency to ignore the callings of the divine self (0) because of a lack of trust in the unfolding of life. This is a pattern of doing to be loved instead of doing what you love. The 5 indicates flexibility issues—being too rigid or too quick to yield. There is a possibility that digestive issues are present.

Asthma (17/8)

The 7 indicates anxiety about making mistakes and being abandoned. There is an associated fear of being judged to be less than we think we are (1). This anxiety can produce rapid and shallow breathing. There are also issues involving frustration or anger, money, personal power, status, and social recognition (8).

Athlete's (27/9) Foot (20/2) = (47/11/2)

With this condition, there is an oversensitivity (11) about making a mistake (7), which leads to procrastination (4). If the left foot is affected, the individual is having difficulty dealing with incoming emotional energy. If it is the right foot, the challenge involves letting go of emotions and anxieties concerning outcomes and moving forward. The final 2 indicates that

the catalyst for this condition always involves interactions with others—
be they physical, emotional, or even energetic—that push "lack of faith
in others" buttons.

Auto (12/3) Immune (30/3) Disorder (47/2) = (89/17/8)

All systems (3—mind, body, spirit) are in disarray due to a loss of confidence (3), causing an inability to accept or hold on to the idea of self-
empowerment (8).

Autoimmune disorders can become chronic (43/7). They develop
as a result of long-term behavior patterns revolving around issues of
abandonment or separation (7), influenced by sub-patterns related to
feelings of inadequacy (3) and stubbornness or constriction (4). The
negative 7 behavior pattern associated with the word *chronic* involves
issues of control, mostly related to who has it, which is different from
the negative 8, which feels disempowered. A negative (chronic) 7 can
also demonstrate a loss of faith, believing that things will never get better and that there's no way out. This type of attitude can drain the life
force from the body. Whatever space was occupied by the life force will
be reoccupied by other forces, such as viruses, bacteria, and molds.

Reading the pattern from the *outside* in—(**89**/17/8), then
(89/**17**/8) and 89/17/**8**—the 8s on either end indicate difficulty with
power issues. Individuals affected by this energy allow themselves to
be disempowered by others when they do not accept their own self-
empowerment. Other issues associated with 8 energy are anger, frustration, money, status, and recognition.

The energy of the negative 9 causes people to do things either to be
loved or to maintain control. Both patterns drain the body's energy and
change its frequency. The change in frequency permits viruses, bacteria,
molds, and fungi to take root, leading to illness and disease. All of the
above descriptions center on actions taken by the ego aspect of the self
to protect itself (1).

The only numbers not included in this disease are 5 and 6. This

```
1 2 3 4 5 6 7 8 9
A B C D E F G H I
J K L M N O P Q R
S T U V W X Y Z
```
Back Pain **77**

implies that the way back to health is to be more flexible (physically, mentally, and emotionally—all issues related to the 5) and to take personal responsibility for one's actions. Healing also comes from becoming more involved in service to the community, energy related to the 6.

B

Illnesses and diseases beginning with the letter B involve issues of sensitivity and dealings with others.

Back (8) Pain (22/4) = (12/3)

Backs are the reservoirs for unreleased emotions, our own and those we hold for others. Back pain tells us that we're carrying too much on our backs and the load needs to be shifted and rebalanced.

Pain is always a signal that something is out of balance at the foundational level (22/4) involving body, mind, or spirit. To ease the pain, the personal issues (22/4) that are the catalysts of the pain need to be identified and dissolved. Here the 22 can also imply a need for the approval of others prior to implementing plans.

Back pain can be caused by a feeling of needing to carry everyone and everything while ignoring our own foundational issues (4). There are abandonment/control issues (4, 8) that are driving these behavior patterns.

If stooping or rounded shoulders are also involved, they indicate trying to hide or withdraw from the world because of lack of confidence (3) or the weight of the carried burdens (2).

Back pain can also be due to the misuse of personal power. For example, fearful (3) of who you could become and what you might have to leave, you pull against the outgoing tide and strain your back. Or, fearful that someone else may "beat you to it," you push against the incoming tide and strain your back.

1	2	3	4	5	6	7	8	9
A	B	C	D	E	F	G	H	I
J	K	L	M	N	O	P	Q	R
S	T	U	V	W	X	Y	Z	

78 Back Problems • Blood Pressure

Back (8) Problems (37/1) = (45/9)

Back problems are caused by being too rigid (5) and controlling (4) and taking on, but not releasing, the woes of others (9). A need to be loved (9) is the underlying cause. The word *problems* (37/1) indicates that they are caused by a need for control (7) due to feelings of inadequacy (3) and a bit of a messianic personality (7). All of this combines to create situations where one becomes an emotional pincushion (9) for others. The soulution is to learn to do what you love (1); stop doing to be loved (8) . . . and let go (9).

Bacterial (35/8) Infection (50/5) = (85/13/4)

The catalyst here is difficulty letting go and making transitions due to feelings of insecurity and inadequacy (13). Also, procrastination (4) is caused by anxieties over what would happen if power was assumed (8). Other possible influences are rigidity (4), inflexibility (5), and frustration (8), coupled with lack of confidence (3) and low self-esteem (1) and culminating in not releasing (4) mental, emotional, or physical wastes. What is not released (13) becomes food (4) for others: in this case, bacteria.

Blood (21/3) Pressure (40/4) = (61/7)

Blood (3) deals with the processes of initiation (1) and cooperation (2), which lead to creation (3). It carries life-giving nutrients throughout our bodies. Notice that the words *high* and *low* both reduce to a 5 and that both high blood pressure and low blood pressure reduce to a 3. The negative interpretation for the number 5 indicates some form of excess behavior; one is either too rigid (type A) or too flexible (type Z).

A negative 3 can produce feelings of inadequacy. Those under its influence can be sarcastic, moody/emotional, introverted, outrageous, withdrawn, passive, boastful, exhibitionists, and "starters" but not "finishers." They can be unforgiving toward those they feel have let them down emotionally.

The total of 61/7 indicates that low self-esteem (1) can be displayed as either arrogance or timidity. The 6 is associated with unrealistic expectations of self or others, leading to issues around control or responsibility. This can manifest as people believing that everything has to be done their way or else it won't work or, at the other extreme, feeling that they shouldn't bother because they'll be blamed for the mistakes of others. This latter attitude is heavily influenced by the negative 7, which, first and foremost, represents abandonment issues and can also indicate anxiety, fear, a need to be needed, and never wanting to be embarrassed or humiliated. Other characteristics of a negative 7 are: overly analytical, totally mental, impatient, manipulative, belittling of others, chronically depressed, distrustful of intuition, having a strong need for control (mental, emotional, physical, spiritual).

▪ **High (32/5) Blood (21/3) Pressure (40/4) = (93/12/3):** This condition tends to affect type-A personalities. Since there are so many 3s and 2s, good communication (3) with others (2) is one of the main problems. Coupling low self-esteem with not trusting emotions or not always communicating in either a timely or appropriate manner (2), the 5 of the word *high* leads to rigidly trying to maintain control of an environment either by allowing emotions free rein (which can be explosive) or by suppressing them (9). This pushing and pulling is a pressurizing force. The tubes carrying the explosive energy of these suppressed emotions can become "over-pressurized" and burst. The number 12 indicates self-esteem issues (1) that result in oversensitivity when dealing with others (2).

See also Hypertension.

▪ **Low (14/5) Blood (21/3) Pressure (40/4) = 75/12/3:** This condition tends to affect type-Z personalities. Individuals with low blood pressure are not good communicators (3), holding things in. Since 5 represents the physical world and 7 the mental world, these individuals have difficulty existing in either world. They want to withdraw (3) from interactions with others (2) and therefore minimize their energy and their exposure (1) to the world. If they withdraw beyond a certain point, the tubes (blood vessels) carrying their life energy can become "under-pressurized" and collapse. The 14/5 of the word *low* indicates individuals who can be overly flexible and give in too easily when interacting with others.

Boil (20/2)

Boils are related to communication issues (2) and difficulty releasing or expressing emotions. Not being released, feelings "boil" to the surface and fester until drained. With the 0 energy, people tend to ignore or not ask for help from Spirit, and try to do everything themselves.

See also Pimple.

Bowels (22/4)

Conditions related to the bowels involve issues of foundation (4), cooperation, communication, and balance when interacting with others (22).

▪ **Bowel Problems (58/13/4):** Foundation issues (22) and a need for approval before making any transitions or letting go (13) are the catalysts for bowel problems. There is a tendency to hold on (4). The 8 deals with power and 5 involves flexibility. This is an individual who tries to hold on to his territory when an external power threatens (8).

▪ **Irritable (49/13/4) Bowel (21/3) Syndrome (41/5) = (111/3):** The 111 represents "I, me, myself." There could be an unforgiving attitude toward the self or others (3), which is expressed with sarcasm, holding on to emotions (9), an inability to let go and move forward (13).

Bruise (29/11/2)

The number 29 signifies emotional tests. This individual is not paying attention to details (2) because of a lack of outward focus. Focus is directed inward due to either emotional issues (9) or difficulty in relationships with others (2). The 11 can indicate a tendency toward self-blame for not being able to make things the way they "should" be. This sets up situations where bruises are the result of pushing against the universe.

Bulimia (31/4) Nervosa (31/4) = (62/8)

In the 62/8, the 2 represents a hypersensitivity to the environment and in interactions with others. The 6 deals with food, relationships, partnerships, obligations, and unrealistic expectations of the self and others. When the 2 and 6 are combined to make 8, we are looking at issues dealing with personal power and status. There is a tendency to be directed out toward the "other" rather than being inner-directed. The challenge is that bulimics (33/6) feel they are letting others down by not meeting some criteria and may martyr themselves by feeling responsible for everyone.

The fact that the words *bulimia* and *nervosa* both transpose numerically to 31/4 reveals that issues of self-esteem (1) and feelings of inadequacy (3) combine to make this individual want to control her environment (4).

C

Illnesses and diseases beginning with the letter C involve issues of communication and feelings of competence.

Cancer (26/8)

Cancer is an 8 and deals with self-empowerment issues. The deeper we bury something, whether it's a dream, an emotion, or a feeling, the more it wants to surface.

The 26 indicates a potential need to be validated by others to relieve abandonment/separation anxieties (7 energy). Adding 2 + 6 + 8, the sum is 16—a karmic number, which reduces to 7 (6 + 1).

Numerically, cancer deals with issues involving money, power, status, recognition, and suppressed anger or frustration. I believe that frustration and anger, resulting from a lack of recognition, aggressive behavior patterns, or feelings of powerlessness—whether related to relationships (2), family (6), or work (8)—are the triggers/catalysts for the various forms of cancer (26/8).

See also Tumor *and* Tumors.

Brain (26/8) Cancer (26/8) = (52/7): With this type of cancer, there is increased *heat* (7) in the cranial cavity due to suppressed anger or emotions (8) related to relationships (2) and responsibilities (6). The 26 signifies that people afflicted with brain cancer have a tendency to keep things to themselves—or in their heads. The 52/7 indicates rigidity (5), sensitivity issues, and poor communication (2) in dealings with others. The 7 shows a need to control situations due to concern over being blamed if anything goes wrong.

Breast (20/2) Cancer (26/8) = (46/1): An oversensitivity (2) to the needs of others (6) combined with needing to be the foundation others can rely on (4) causes a suppression of the self (1) for the sake of a relationship or family (6).

Breast cancer occurs more often in women than in men and it is located near the heart. Women offer their breasts to nurture those they love, whether a husband, partner, children, relatives, friends, or coworkers. When they are drained dry and those they care for don't seem any happier, women may feel there is something wrong with them since they can't seem to satisfy their loved ones' emotional needs. Rather than assuming blame for some imaginary lack of ability to mother or nurture, the first thing to realize is that the individuals being nurtured are not recipients of love but takers of energy. Their emotional needs can never be satisfied by another because they don't have the awareness or trust to appreciate the support available to them.

Breast cancer is a result of suppressed feelings and emotions related to not being acknowledged for who you are and what you do. The lump (8) of cancer (8) is the encapsulation of these suppressed feelings and emotions. In this case, the release point is the breast. For a woman, this is a point of nurturing and the offering of sustenance. If the nurturing or sustenance is not acknowledged or appreciated by others, energy particles with a positive charge can be overwhelmed by negatively charged particles. This leads to inflammation (1) of the area and the process of contracting the illness begins. To reverse the process, the individual needs to begin honoring the self and doing what she loves, rather than acting in order to be loved or to maintain control.

■ **Cervical (37/1) Cancer (26/8) = (63/9):** Similar to breast cancer, cervical cancer is the result of a suppression of the self (1). The ovaries, womb, uterus, cervix, vagina, bladder, and kidneys are all places where women hide or stuff their emotions (9) and personal power (8). Over a long period of time, the concentrated energy of these emotions generates a tremendous amount of heat, which alters the chemical balance and allows for cellular changes. It is this heat that kills off the "normal" cells, allowing "abnormal" cells to take root. Candida infections have the same characteristics.

The 37/1 combination indicates issues involving abandonment and control (7) combined with feelings of inadequacy and poor communication skills (3), which leaves these individuals with low self-esteem (1).

The number combination of 63/9 also indicates that this illness is associated with feelings of inadequacy (3) as well as a need for relationships (6) and a need to be loved (9).

Cervical cancer can be associated with personality types that internalize and repress their aspirations, hopes, dreams, and sense of self (3) in exchange for a relationship that offers them security (6). These individuals may live their life to be loved (9). Another associated personality type seeks physical acceptance through relationships (6) due to feelings

84   Cancer (Colon)

1	2	3	4	5	6	7	8	9
A	B	C	D	E	F	G	H	I
J	K	L	M	N	O	P	Q	R
S	T	U	V	W	X	Y	Z	

of insecurity and inadequacy (3). They, too, would live their lives either to be loved (9) or to maintain emotional control of relationships (9).

See also Human Papillomavirus Infection *and* Squamous Cell Carcinoma.

The next three descriptions (colon, colorectal, and kidney cancer) all contain the number 13, a number that requires individuals to let go of the past and move into the future. It is a number that requires constant transition. The negative 13/4 can be stubborn, skeptical, and controlling (4) due to underlying feelings of inadequacy (3) and low self-esteem (1). The personalities of these individuals are of a similar nature—all demonstrate a constrictive or "holding on to" behavior pattern. They choose not to release their emotional wastes, which become nourishment for viral (8) life-forms.

■ **Colon (23/5) Cancer (26/8) = (49/13/4):** The letters *c* and *o* of *colon* added together equal 9 and subtracted equal 3. This 9/3 combination indicates individuals who can be unforgiving toward those who don't appreciate their compassionate nature—somewhat of an oxymoron. If you are compassionate, you don't need to be recognized as compassionate; you are.

The issue with colon cancer is flexibility, release, and movement (5). The 23 indicates difficulty maintaining harmony and balance (2) within the body due to withdrawal or pulling back of emotions because of uncertainties (3) that feed feelings of inadequacy.

When looking at the 49/13/4 combination, we can see that control issues associated with the 4, along with an inability to release emotions (9), make it difficult for this individual to release feelings or emotions and move on (13). The 4 appears at both ends of the equation, indicating an individual who must be in control. The energy of control is constrictive and can exhaust the defenses of the body. Like children being potty trained, if we want to control (4) the perceived controller, we withhold our bowel movement; we refuse to release our emotional wastes.

```
1 2 3 4 5 6 7 8 9
A B C D E F G H I
J K L M N O P Q R
S T U V W X Y Z
```
Cancer (Colorectal) • Cancer (Liver) **85**

▪ **Colorectal (41/5) Cancer (26/8) = (67/13/4):** The overriding issues with colorectal cancer are related to flexibility and movement (5). The 41 indicates low self-esteem (1), which can make this individual stubborn and a bit of a reactionary (both are associated with 4).

The 67/13/4 combination shows perfectionist tendencies or unrealistic expectations (6) as well as anxiety about being misunderstood by others and being abandoned or humiliated (7). This is also associated with a need for control because *"no one can do it as well as I can"* (7). This combination makes it difficult to let go of waste material (i.e., what was) and move on (13). The single-digit 4 indicates that we are dealing with foundational issues. The internal structure, or foundation, of the colon is not smooth or solid; it is riddled with pockets of self-doubt.

▪ **Kidney (32/5) Cancer (26/8) = (58/13/4):** The kidney is both a filter of and a repository for emotions and wastes. The catalysts for kidney cancer are holding on to negative emotions (2) and a failure to communicate feelings (3), which can lead to a rigid (5) emotional state or a shutting down of the release valve, thus causing a backup of wastes.

The 58/13/4 combination defines an attitude that is inflexible (5), frustrated, or angry (8), with low self-esteem (1) and feelings of inadequacy (3) making it difficult to let go (13) of control (4).

▪ **Liver (30/3) Cancer (26/8) = (56/11/2):** Like the kidneys, the liver is both a filter of and a repository for our emotions. The main issues associated with the liver are feelings of inadequacy, lack of emotional intimacy, and difficulty expressing and/or releasing emotions, all related to negative 3 energy.

Looking at the combination of 56/11/2, I want to first talk about the 11—the first master number and, as such, one of the hardest numbers to work with. The 11 allows one to see the way things ought to be but brings forth frustration over being unable to make them that way. The 5 represents difficulty with changes. The individual with liver cancer feels responsible (6) for others and may mentally beat himself up for being unable to make things right (according to his own definition) for others (2).

◾ **Lung (18/9) Cancer (26/8) = (44/8):** Lung cancer metastasizes through the lymphatic (44) system and/or the bloodstream (43/7). Ninety percent of lung cancer is found in smokers. Numerically, the word *smokers* is a 28/1, indicating passive-aggressive personality patterns associated with feelings of insecurity (1). Smoking (34/7) deals with control issues (4 and 7) combined with feelings of inadequacy (3) or abandonment issues.

The main issue associated with the lungs is a failure to release emotions (9). The 8 indicates feeling that personal empowerment is being constricted. There can also be unexpressed concerns about status, money, and power. The 1 deals with self-esteem issues.

The power number 44 calls for drawing a line in the sand and "taking a stand." Lung cancer is about learning to overcome procrastination (4) and control issues (4) by the *right* use and acceptance of personal power (8) and the release of anger or frustrations (8).

◾ **Lymphatic (44/8) Cancer (26/8) = (70/7):** One of the primary functions of the lymphatic system is to remove and destroy toxic substances and fight the spread of disease in the body. The 8 indicates that suppressed anger and frustration are being disseminated throughout the body via the lymphatic system.

The 44, in this instance, indicates that stubbornness (4) and procrastination (4) are a part of the personality pattern. These individuals can be fearful and hesitate when making decisions (4), or their decisions are made to maintain control. They will, at some point in their lives, be called upon to stand up for what they believe (44). If they come from their hearts and stand their ground, they will step into personal empowerment (8). If not, they will continue to interact with others based on their need to be loved or needed, or based on their need to remain in control (7).

Lymphatic cancer (70/7) manifests as a result of abandonment

1	2	3	4	5	6	7	8	9
A	B	C	D	E	F	G	H	I
J	K	L	M	N	O	P	Q	R
S	T	U	V	W	X	Y	Z	

Cancer (Ovarian) • Cancer (Prostate) **87**

issues (7) and lack of support in daily interactions, whether it's with others or with Spirit (0). These feelings lead to concerns over being in control of one's environment (7). Letting go of the perception of being a victim is essential for healing.

■ **Ovarian (35/8) Cancer (26/8) = (61/7):** The pelvic area (ovaries, womb, uterus, cervix, vagina) is a place where women hide or stuff their emotions. Over a long period of time, the emotions generate tremendous amounts of heat, which kills off the "normal" cells and gives "abnormal" cells a place to take root. Candida infections have the same characteristics.

Here again, the issue is about power (8). In this case, it is about allowing one's power to be constrained (5) by others due to feelings of inadequacy. This can lead to moodiness and a failure to communicate feelings (3). The 61/7 combination indicates an individual whose self-esteem (1) is tied to doing for others (6) because of a strong need to be needed or to maintain control (7). The number 6 can also indicate unrealistic expectations of self and others.

■ **Pancreatic (45/9) Cancer (26/8) = (71/8) / Adenocarcinoma of the Exocrine Glands (159/15/6):** The main issues for these conditions are dealing with emotions (9), inflexibility (5), and control (4). Secondary issues include abandonment anxiety (7); low self-esteem (1); and the use, misuse, or abuse of personal power (8).

The 159/15/6 combination indicates emotional rigidity (9), inflexibility (5), and low self-esteem (1). The numbers for inflexibility (5) and low self-esteem (1) appear twice. The negative 6 reveals difficulty with relationships, partnerships, obligations, responsibilities, and unrealistic expectations for self and others. This affects blood sugar levels (63/9), which returns us to feelings of inadequacy (3) in relationships (6) and causing a "stuffing" of emotions (9).

■ **Prostate (33/6) Cancer (26/8) = (59/14/5):** Here we see issues of responsibility—taking on too much (33)—along with unrealistic

88   Cancer (Skin)

1	2	3	4	5	6	7	8	9
A	B	C	D	E	F	G	H	I
J	K	L	M	N	O	P	Q	R
S	T	U	V	W	X	Y	Z	

expectations of self and others. A tendency to hold on to things and constrictive behavior patterns cause the prostate to swell.

The 59/14/5 combination indicates a rigid attitude (with 5s on either end) involving emotions (9) and control (4) of all things related to the self (1). The number 14 indicates a pattern of being too rigid or, in some cases, too flexible in dealings with others.

⬚ **Skin (17/8) Cancer (26/8) = (26/8) = (43/7):** Whatever emotions (3) individuals try to suppress or control (4) due to fears of abandonment (7) will find their way to the surface. Most people have a tendency to *overexpose* themselves. If they are doing something to be loved, thanked, or appreciated, they have a tendency to "hang around" a little too long. If they are doing something to enable them to maintain control of a situation, they "hold on" too long. The 8 total of both *skin* and *cancer* reveals additional issues concerning status, appearance, power, and recognition.

The location on the body where the skin cancer manifests can give additional insight into the possible causes of the disease. Cancer of the nose (70/7), for instance, could be related to micromanaging (7). Some people have a pattern of defiantly "poking their nose where it doesn't belong" whether it is in the sun or in someone else's life; they are looking for validation (8) of their importance to the group.

Different types of skin cancer have specific energies and behavior patterns associated with them:

> **Basal (8) Cell (14/5) Carcinoma (41/5) = (63/9):** Triggers for this type of skin cancer (in the bottom layer of the epidermis) involve suppressed anger or frustration (8) and the storage of excess emotions (14 and 9) under the surface, at the cellular level. A feeling of inadequacy or a lack of communication (3) in relationships (6) is also involved and leads to suppressed emotions (9) looking for a way to the surface.

> **Melanoma (34/7):** The most deadly of the skin cancers, the numbers for melanoma are a repeat of the numbers for skin cancer

```
1 2 3 4 5 6 7 8 9
A B C D E F G H I
J K L M N O P Q R
S T U V W X Y Z
```
Cancer (Spinal) • Cancer (Stomach) **89**

(43/7). Again, whatever emotions (3) we try to suppress or control (4), due to fears of abandonment (7) and feelings of inadequacy, will find their way to the surface.

Squamous (27/9) Cell (14/5) Carcinoma (41/5) = (82/1): The individual with this type of skin cancer (in the upper layer of the epidermis) has difficulty dealing with changes involving others (2) due to abandonment issues (7). Emotionally, they can be either flat or bombastic (9). There is a tendency toward rigidity (the 14 and 41 both reduce to a 5) associated with communication issues (2), personal power (8), and self-esteem (1). There is the possibility that this individual could be passive-aggressive or aggressive-passive, based on the final number, 82/1.

Spinal (26/8) Cancer (26/8) = (52/7): The basic issues associated with spinal cancer are nerves (2), unrealistic expectations in relation to responsibilities (6), and a stubbornness or stiffness (8) radiating through the nervous system. The spine is to the nervous system as the brain is to bodily functions. The spine (9) holds the emotions for the body and acts as a clearinghouse. If emotions are not released and dispersed, the spine and its accompanying nerves are overwhelmed and the negativity leaks into the body.

Spinal cancer can result from weak communication skills (2) that can cause one to become either very rigid or overly amenable (5). In either case, the underlying motive is the 7 and its fear of rejection or abandonment. These underlying fears are so great that they can lead to paralysis of the system. The subconscious rationale may be "If I can't move, they can't leave me. They have to take care of me."

Stomach (25/7) Cancer (26/8) = (51/6): Stomach cancer shares many of the basic patterns as spinal cancer: rigidity (5), difficulty interacting with others (2), and an internalization of anxieties concerning abandonment issues (7). Stomach cancer occurs in the area of the third chakra, the energetic area of the body associated with self-empowerment. The

90 Cancer (Testicular) • Cancer (Throat)

1	2	3	4	5	6	7	8	9
A	B	C	D	E	F	G	H	I
J	K	L	M	N	O	P	Q	R
S	T	U	V	W	X	Y	Z	

core issues with this type of cancer involve self-esteem (1), flexibility (5), and unrealistic expectations of self and others (6). The number 6 is also associated with love, family, community, food, and codependency issues.

▪ **Testicular (38/11/2) Cancer (26/8) = 64/10/1:** The 64/10/1 total describes a perfectionist (6) who can become lost in the details (4) trying to make everything perfect. For many people under the influence of the 6, if they cannot complete something to their satisfaction, they will procrastinate, get lost in the details, or quit (4). This can make them stubborn (4), even arrogant (1), to cover a lack of self-confidence (1). The 10 represents trying to do it alone (1) rather than working in partnership with the universe.

I'm certain that many male readers will identify with this picture: When a male driver hits a deep pothole, there is usually a knee-jerk reaction of drawing the testicles upward, almost as though there was a fear of being castrated. It is this same anxiety that causes some individuals to hold themselves back (reflected in the 1 total).

Individuals with testicular cancer may have held themselves back (8) because of underlying feelings of inadequacy (rooted in the number 11). Eleven is the first of the master numbers and also the most frustrating. It allows one's higher self to see the way things are but not the ego (physical self). Since the ego is not privy to this "view," it will sabotage whatever pushes its abandonment-issue buttons. It will continue to try to shape reality as it thinks it ought to be. There is no partnership (2) with the higher self (0). In order to begin the healing process, the ego (1) must form a partnership either with Spirit (0) or with others (2), but preferably with Spirit.

▪ **Throat (28/1) Cancer (26/8) = (54/9):** The number 28 can represent passive-aggressive behavior patterns. The 2 deals with cooperation and timely communication while the 8 calls for being true to the self and not suppressing anger or frustration. The combination calls for an individual to speak out (2) assertively (8) without fearing rejection from others (1).

The 54/9 combination indicates a tendency to not speak up or to express only anger or frustration. It indicates that emotions and concern over not being loved, recognized, or appreciated can cause this individual to become rigid (5) and hold on to (4) negative emotions (9). There is anxiety over speaking one's "heart truth" stemming from fear of abandonment.

Candida (27/9) Infection (50/5) = (77/14/5)

The main issues concern holding in emotions (2 and 9) or becoming enmeshed in other people's (2) emotions (9) as well as being reactive rather than proactive in communications (2). It's also about control and who has it. If a person is "doing" to make others happy, she is not in control; she is being controlled (9). Notice that the 77/14/5 total has two 7s: these behavior patterns can be attributed to abandonment issues associated with the number 7.

The 77/14/5 total indicates individuals who have a tendency to spread themselves too thin trying to "do" for everyone (14)—not only because they "know" their way is better (1) but also because they feel a need to do everything themselves (1) to avoid mistakes. If they don't do it "all," they become anxious over the possibility of being blamed for another's mistake (7) and then abandoned (7) as a result. Since the final 5 is a distillation of both the 77 (7 + 7 = 14) and the 14, the big issue is balance. Candida cannot get a foothold if individuals are living a balanced life. This includes balance in diet as well as in mental, emotional, physical, and spiritual aspects.

The itching associated with the infection is one way of breaking control patterns. How can you not scratch an itch? Attention is being directed to an unrecognized irritation.

The first (1) and second (2) chakras are also involved with this condition. The first chakra holds survival, self-preservation, and life-force energies. The second chakra is the seat of sexuality, involvement with others, and procreation (birthing). A candida infection may provide an excuse for not having to engage in unwanted sexual activity, a way of getting back some personal power.

The *c* and *a* of *candida* can be added together for a sum of 4 and subtracted with a remainder of 2. This 4/2 combination can indicate a desire to maintain order, system, structure, and a schedule. There is a perception that others are inconsistent and cannot be trusted to complete a task appropriately; therefore, these individuals try to do it all themselves. It's about control and abandonment (7).

Again, the 27/9 reinforces this by revealing a pattern of holding on to an emotion or having a sentimental attachment (2) to someone or something because of anxieties and concerns about being alone (7). The 9 indicates a pattern of either "doing to be loved" or "doing to maintain control."

See also Autoimmune Disorder.

Carpal (24/6) Tunnel (23/5) Syndrome (41/5) = (88/16/7)

This condition deals with responsibilities (6) in the physical world (5). In this instance, the 41/5 represents the individual (1) in the workplace (4) and issues of flexibility (5).

The main concern is expressed through the number 16, which represents "forcing an issue." With carpal tunnel syndrome, the body has been forced to perform unnatural motions on a repetitive basis.

The double 8s represent authority and its control over the individual (1). The individual with this condition feels the responsibility (6) of family or dependents and therefore fears abandonment (7) by or separation from the employer/authority. There is a tendency to not speak up (2) in a timely manner in the workplace.

Cerebral (37/1) Palsy (19/1) = (56/11/2)

The overriding issue with this condition is an individual's inability to find her center within the body (19/1). Cerebral palsy affects both lobes (2) of the brain. The palsy is an imbalance in the electrical field

1	2	3	4	5	6	7	8	9
A	B	C	D	E	F	G	H	I
J	K	L	M	N	O	P	Q	R
S	T	U	V	W	X	Y	Z	

Chronic Fatigue Syndrome   **93**

between positive- and negative-charged particles (19), causing a fluctuation in the flow, which accentuates opposite extremes. All of this is a result of the 11. Being the first master number, the 11 enables the individual to "see" the way things could be; however, frustration resulting from the realization that she cannot *make* it that way leads to an imbalance (2) between the soul and the physical self. The 5 indicates change and the 6 relates that change to the family situation.

Chronic (43/7) Fatigue (33/6) Syndrome (41/5) = (117/9)

The numbers indicate that these individuals have had a need to maintain control or have been driven by a need to be thanked, appreciated, recognized, or loved for their actions—either path represents negative 9 behaviors and is related to abandonment issues (7). The 117 indicates that these individuals sustain their identity by becoming *doers for* or *controllers of* others out of a need to be loved (9).

■ **Chronic (43/7) Fatigue (33/6) = (76/13/4):** Looking at just the two words, *chronic* and *fatigue,* we see that these individuals are body tired from focusing on the needs of others. The 76/13/4 combination indicates that this is related to lack of self-acceptance and self-imposed feelings of inadequacy (3). These feelings can lead to procrastination or stubbornness (4) and a state of physical exhaustion (7). There is also a tendency to commit to "doing for others" to the point of martyrdom (33/6), thereby depleting the sense of self (1). The 7 indicates needing to be in control due to anxieties about abandonment and vulnerability. Trying to maintain control is very tiring.

The 13 is a karmic number indicating a pattern of stubbornness associated with feelings of inadequacy, low self-esteem, and the need to be in control. The 13 also indicates difficulty letting go and moving on. A core challenge for those with chronic fatigue is learning to release their grip and accept the uncertainty of life and relationships.

Cirrhosis (55/1)

Cirrhosis is usually the result of alcoholism (44/8), when individuals are unable to stand up for their beliefs. Grandiosity and procrastination (44) lead to anger (8), which may be internalized or externalized. There are also issues involving personal power (8)—individuals either abuse their power or are fearful of stepping into their power.

Individuals with cirrhosis are caught between wanting to move forward and remaining frozen in the moment (both inclinations are associated with the number 5); they have lost their sense of direction and do not know which way is forward (1).

Another interpretation is that an absolute refusal to change (55) and move forward (1) leads to stagnation, and live liver cells are replaced by dead ones.

Cold (16/7)

A karmic number indicating a messianic behavior pattern, the 16 indicates that individuals suffering from colds feel personally responsible for making certain that there are no mistakes so that their image remains intact and unchallenged (7). This illness often occurs during a time when responsibility can seem overwhelming (6), causing self-esteem issues to arise (1). This can lead to "forcing the issue" (16), which results in a form of paralysis that forces individuals to stop what they are doing (7). The numeric energy of a cold reminds people to let go (7). It brings about a state of being incapacitated (7) in some way—physically, mentally, or emotionally—and provides time to investigate the lesson to be learned (7).

Here are interpretations for some of the common symptoms associated with colds:

▪ **Congestion (49/13/4):** Congestion indicates a pattern of stubbornly (4) holding on to emotional attachments and not being able to let go of emotional issues (9). The 13 represents difficulty dealing with transitions; coupled with the 9 and the final 4, there is a direct link with abandonment anxieties and the need to remain in control. The message here is to let go, release, and move on!

▪ **Cough (27/9):** With a cough, the body is trying to forcibly rid itself (9) of unspoken (2) anxieties (7) and emotions (9).

▪ **Coughing (48/12/3):** Coughing is a repetitive pattern adopted by the mind/body to bring to the surface suppressed communications (3) that involve self (1) and others (2) and are related to work (4) and relationships (2). The 48 indicates procrastination (4) as a result of not wanting to accept personal power (8) or feeling overwhelmed by financial issues. The more intense the cough, the deeper the emotion is buried. Communicating feelings and emotional intimacy can help mediate the severity of a cough.

▪ **Sinus (19/1):** Sinus problems result from emotional (9) issues that involve the self (1) and others not being dealt with. There is apprehension that the outcome will have a negative impact, so emotions are not expressed and begin to fill the sinus cavities.

▪ **Sneeze (29/11/2):** Many people try to contain a sneeze to minimize the sound and avoid embarrassment, making noise, or disturbing others (2). A sneeze manifests when something from somewhere is not being expressed in a timely manner. The sneeze is a way for the individual to call attention to himself and clear the body of restrained feelings or emotions (9).

▪ **Sniffles (36/9):** When someone has the sniffles, a feeling of inadequacy or a desire to avoid confrontation (3) within interpersonal relationships (6) has caused emotions to be held back, unexpressed. As the emotions dribble out through the nose, there is a tendency to try to suck them back.

▪ **Sore (21/3) Throat (28/1) = (49/13/4):** The catalyst for a sore throat is not communicating (3) feelings or opinions, which creates an irritation with self (1) or others (2). The 28/1 indicates an abrogation of personal power (1 and 8) due to oversensitivity to the feelings of others (2).

The 49/13/4 total indicates that a sore throat is associated with difficulty making transitions (13) and overcoming stubbornness or procrastination (4) in interactions with others. The 9 identifies an underlying pattern of either not speaking up because of a desire to be loved or speaking too much because of a need to be in control.

Colic (24/6)

Issues associated with colic are related to family (6) and/or the digestive system (66). This condition deals with the foundational issues of the number 4 (e.g., food and nurturing) and parent/child (2) communication.

The *c* and *o* of *colic* can be added together for a sum of 9 and subtracted with a remainder of 3; this is read as a 9/3 combination. This individual may be attempting to communicate emotional needs or be demonstrating a need for love and attention due to feelings of inadequacy.

Colitis (33/6)

With this condition, perfectionist tendencies, high expectations for self or others, underlying feelings of inadequacy, and an inclination toward taking on too much responsibility directly impact the digestive system. Colitis also indicates an imbalance in the area of the third chakra, the area of self-empowerment.

With the number 33, there is major martyrdom involved. People with colitis are "doers" and make themselves indispensable so that no one can make do without them. Even if they don't want to do something in their hearts, they will do it anyway out of a need to be needed or because they don't want to see others suffer.

There is an uncontrolled innate desire to help and nurture associated with this disease. The big lesson for those with colitis is to make themselves their first priority: Heal thyself, then mentor others through their changes.

Constipation (56/11/2)

Constipation is linked with holding back and not speaking up in a timely manner (2). There's a touch of rigidity (5) mixed with unrealistic expectations (6) of the way life ought to be (11). This leads to withdrawal (2) or withholding of energy.

Crohn's (32/5) Disease (26/8) = (58/13/4)

The primary issue is oversensitivity in interactions with others (2) coupled with feelings of inadequacy (3), which can lead to a pattern of doing for others only to maintain peace, indicating some form of codependency. Learning to honor the self is the only way to break this pattern.

The 58/13/4 combination indicates an avoidance of personal power (8), appearing overly amenable (5), and an inability to transition out (13) of current behavior patterns. With 4 as the final number, Crohn's disease manifests as a result of clinging (4) to others for support instead of solidifying the foundation of self.

The symptoms of Crohn's disease include diarrhea, abdominal pain, possible weight loss, and fever. Each of these symptoms involves releasing. Diarrhea can be an uncontrollable release of wastes. Abdominal pain (associated with the third chakra area) calls attention to stuffed emotions or emotional wastes that need to be released. Weight loss is the body's method of ridding itself of the ego's accumulated expectations of the way things ought to be, and fever is the body's way of burning off excessive emotional clutter.

Cystitis (34/7)

Cystitis is an inflammation (1) of the bladder (8). This condition calls attention to foundational issues (4). The bladder is a storage facility, storing (3) anger and frustration, among other things, and cystitis is associated with learning how to express those feelings. The message is to let go of self-imposed restrictions (4); communicate feelings (3); and release any fears of rejection, embarrassment, or abandonment (7).

In speaking with women, there appears to be a correlation between engaging in sexual activity with a partner they don't feel like having sex with and developing cystitis. There's apprehension about ending the relationship or frustration associated with a lack of respect or feelings of inadequacy. These women think that maybe the relationship would work if they tried harder to keep their partner happy.

See also Urinary Tract Infection.

Cysts (14/5)

Cysts are nodules of excess (14) negative energy or "toxins," created by stubbornness (4) and low self-esteem (1). The rigidity of the negative 5 provides the cysts a means for assuming a physical form.

See also Ovarian Cysts.

D

Illnesses and diseases that begin with the letter *D* involve issues of control and dependability.

Dementia (35/8)

These individuals have had a rigid outlook on life (5), have not always expressed themselves (3), and have needed to be in control and "run the show" (8). The *de,* as the first consonant/first vowel combination, indicates a pattern of doing to be loved or to maintain control. As a result of dementia, these individuals must now relinquish control and allow others to do for them.

Depression (52/7)

Difficulty communicating feelings, oversensitivity (2), and an inability to move forward (5) can lead to a sort of mental, emotional, or physical paralysis (7). Depressed individuals may feel they have not received sufficient recognition for their "contributions" or that they have no control (7) over the events of their lives. They may feel that it is not worth trying since they will ultimately fail and be rejected (7). They feel abandoned by the universe (7) and separated from others (2), which leads to an inability to move forward mentally, emotionally, or physically (5).

Diabetes (29/11/2)

The main issue associated with diabetes is hypersensitivity (2) to the feelings and emotions (9) of others (2) at the expense of self (1). The hypersensitivity is linked to the number 11, which, as the first of the master numbers, is also the most frustrating. It allows one to see the way things ought to be but does not provide the power or opportunity to make the necessary changes. As a result, self-esteem suffers and the individual may either cease communicating feelings altogether or become overly aggressive in communicating them (beating people over the head with a steel bar of truth). There is also the issue of not being understood by partners, parents, family, or the world at large.

See also Hypoglycemia.

▪ **Type I (20/2) or Insulin-Dependent Diabetes Mellitus:** Type I diabetes is considered to be an autoimmune (42/6) disease (26/8) because the immune system attacks and destroys cells in the pancreas, known as beta cells (25/7). These cells are responsible for producing insulin (35/8).

Type I diabetes has associated partnership/relationship/communication issues (2). Timely communication, indicated by the prevalence of 2s associated with this condition (20, 2, 42, 25), is also a core issue. There is also an associated need for control (4 and 7) coupled with unrealistic expectations of self or others (6). Additionally, the numbers related to this disease reveal a pattern of self-imposed rigidity (5) associated with feelings of inadequacy (3) and anxiety over being abandoned (7). Ultimately, the individual constricts or suppresses personal power (8).

1	2	3	4	5	6	7	8	9
A	B	C	D	E	F	G	H	I
J	K	L	M	N	O	P	Q	R
S	T	U	V	W	X	Y	Z	

100   Diabetes (Type II) • Ear Problems

■ **Type II (21/3) or Non-Insulin-Dependent Diabetes Mellitus:** Type II diabetes, in which the body either makes insufficient amounts of insulin (35/8) or is unable to use it (2), accounts for 90 to 95 percent of all cases of diagnosed diabetes in the United States.

The issues for this condition revolve around low self-esteem (1), hypersensitivity to others, codependency, and not speaking up in a timely manner (2). This individual has created self-imposed limitations due to feelings of inadequacy and the perception of being ignored (3). There is difficulty tasting and digesting the sweetness (3) of life.

Drug Problems (60/6)

Those with drug problems face issues of personal responsibility and unrealistic expectations of self and others, which leads to disappointment and a desire to escape the current reality. There are issues of anxiety and difficulty involving "close" relationships with others (6).

The abuse of a drug (23/5) is the result of poor communication skills (2), feelings of inadequacy (3), and an inability to function in the physical world (5) due to unrealistic expectations (6).

See also under Addictions.

E

Illnesses and diseases beginning with the letter *E* are birthed in the nervous system.

Ear (15/6) Problems (37/1) = (52/7)

The underlying issues with ear problems involve not feeling in control and not wanting to hear (5) or listen (7) to what others (2) have to say. Another possibility is that hearing what others (2) have to say could be very upsetting (5).

■ **Earache (32/5):** The issue is not wanting to hear (23/5) and, by default, not wanting to deal with or accept what others (2) are saying. The underlying catalysts are a feeling of inadequacy (3) and a need to be more present and flexible (5).

Eczema (26/8)

Perceived expectations about outcomes involving self and others (6), with little or no interpersonal communication (2), can generate frustration (8) and anger. A withholding or stifling of personal power (8) can cause negative energy trapped under the skin to force its way to the surface as lesions, scales, or pustules. Once there, they can form protective scales or crusts, which keep others from getting close.

Adding and subtracting the numeric values of the first two letters of *eczema* (*e* = 5 and *c* =3) gives a result of 8/2. This 8/2 combination of *ec* indicates poor communication skills due to individuals expecting that people should know what is wanted of them without having to be told. When the results are not what was expected, these individuals can become angry and/or frustrated.

The 26/8 total reinforces the pattern of unrealistic expectations of others (6) along with poor communication and people skills (2). It also indicates a tendency to bully or verbally abuse others (8). If this is the case, rage, anger, and/or frustrations rise to the surface and harden as a manifestation of a hardened attitude.

The 26/8 can also indicate a hypersensitivity to the needs of others (2), creating a pattern of taking on responsibility (6) for others (2). This is done out of apprehension or anxiety associated with having to leave others to "step into their power" (8) along with a need to be recognized for a compassionate (6) nature.

The last letter of *eczema* is an *a*. Whenever *a* appears as the last letter of a name or illness, it is an indication that one of the catalysts for negative situations was not trusting one's intuition or listening to the inner self.

Edema (19/1)

The letters *e* and *d* added together equal 9 and subtracted equal 1. This 9/1 combination is a repeat of the 19 of *edema*. This repetition indicates that the self (1) is torn between doing and not wanting to do for others—but ultimately "does" anyway. The push/pull between the masculine (1) and feminine (9), between moving forward and standing still, creates friction. The heat generated from this friction causes unreleased emotions (9) to condense into a fluid (25/7). This 7 represents issues of personal control and anxiety about being abandoned if the truth is spoken.

Endometriosis (66/12/3)

The 66 represents the main catalyst for this health issue: an overwhelming sense of needing to nurture, which comes from an identity (1) that has been based on the need to be needed by others (2). The total of 3 indicates that this pattern is the result of self-imposed feelings of inadequacy and difficulty expressing feelings concerning emotional intimacy.

The pelvic area (ovaries, womb, uterus, cervix, and vagina) is a place where women hide or stuff their emotions (9). Over a long period of time, these emotions generate tremendous amounts of heat, which kills off the "normal" cells and gives "abnormal" cells a place to take root. The physical pain (4) associated with endometriosis is a signal to look at the foundation of the personality. How strong are feelings of inadequacy (3)? Are emotional attachments (2)—whether to people, things, or memories—being held on to or released? Does pleasing another determine the action to be taken (6)?

Enuresis (38/11/2)

Emotions and frustrations that are held in while the individual is conscious (3 and 8) escape during unconsciousness. At night, when the mind relaxes and releases, so does the body and thus bed-wetting may occur. The 11, being a master number, indicates knowledge of the way things are "supposed" to be but does not grant the power (8) to make things that way.

Eye Blinking (59/14/5)

Eye blinking indicates a state of nervousness derived from excess energy (from the 5s on either end of the 59/14/5 combination) and uncertainty (1) about what's happening (5) in the environment. The excess energy is reinforced by the 14, a number indicating excessiveness (too much or too little) in personal actions—for instance, trying to process too much information in too short a time. The 9 deals with the uncertainties associated with being loved by those around you; the 4 indicates that in times of uncertainty, the self (1) can be stubborn.

> ## F
>
> Illnesses and diseases beginning with the letter *F* are associated with a need to do for others in an effort to control them.

Fibromyalgia (64/1)

Those with fibromyalgia feel a need to maintain control (4) of or for their social unit. There may be an associated touch of martyrdom (6) due to unrealistic expectations (6) stemming from self-esteem issues (1). The associated behavior pattern is based on the belief that no one can perform to this individual's level of satisfaction (6). As a result, the individual takes full responsibility/control (4)—not just in one area but in every aspect of her life as well. This pattern exhausts the entire body, which is why chronic fatigue also occurs. (*See also* Chronic Fatigue.)

It's interesting that one of the tests for fibromyalgia is to touch eighteen points on the body to see if there is pain or discomfort associated with the touching. If eleven of these points respond with pain,

$$\begin{array}{ccccccccc} 1 & 2 & 3 & 4 & 5 & 6 & 7 & 8 & 9 \\ A & B & C & D & E & F & G & H & I \\ J & K & L & M & N & O & P & Q & R \\ S & T & U & V & W & X & Y & Z \end{array}$$

104   Flatulence • Fungus Infection

fibromyalgia can be diagnosed. The number 18 reduces to a 9, which represents emotions and the need to be either loved, recognized, or appreciated or to maintain emotional control of relationships. The number 11, the first of the master numbers, brings frustration associated with knowing the way things ought to be but being unable to make them that way. As a result, the individual absorbs *blame,* which transposes to a 6.

Flatulence (36/9)
The 6 refers to food or sustenance and the word *digestion* reduces to the number 3. The 9 indicates a need to let go. The expelling of gas is the result of trying to hold in things out of a fear of rejection.

Flu (12/3)
Unspoken emotions (3) relating to others (2) impacts how we feel about ourselves (1). The flu indicates disappointment (3) in not being recognized, appreciated, thanked, or loved by others. This combination can also indicate a desire to withdraw (3) from society.
    See also Cold *and* Influenza.

Frigidity (62/8)
Communication issues (2) combined with perfectionist tendencies (6) result in power issues (8): Who's in charge? Who has the power? The numbers 2 and 6 also deal with relationships and issues of vulnerability.

Fungus (25/7) Infection (50/5) = (75/12/3)
For those with fungus infections, mind (7) and body (5) have become caught in a pattern of low self-esteem (1) and not communicating (2) feelings because of fear or anxiety over what may occur if they did express themselves or move forward (5) with their lives. The 3 represents self-imposed feelings of inadequacy, scattered energy, pessimism, and a desire to withdraw from "the field of play" (associated with athlete's foot).

> ## G
> Illnesses and diseases beginning with the letter G are associated with a need to be in control whether in relationships or at work. There can also be a need to release thoughts, feelings, or emotions.

Gallstones (34/7)

Gallstones are directly linked with bile. Numerically, *bile* is a 19/1, indicating that if an individual continually swings between displaying a sweet and a sour attitude, there will be an irregular flow of bile. This irregularity can be linked with procrastination, being an obstructionist (4), or having an unforgiving attitude (3). These behavior patterns stem from a fear of being rejected or humiliated (7). A hardening of attitude can of itself manifest gallstones.

Gastritis (41/5), Chronic (43/7) = (84/12/3)

The *gas* of gastritis equals 9, which is always associated with the emotions. In gastritis, an inflammation (1) initiated by unresolved emotions causes the stomach lining to break down (associated with the 4, which represents issues of foundation). The stomach fails in its attempt to digest the emotional issues. The 84/12/3 combination indicates that the foundation (4) of the illness lies with issues surrounding money, power, recognition, and status (8). These issues stem from the 1, which represents a compromised sense of self and passivity or aggression when dealing with others (2). The negative 3 is associated with awkward social interactions; low self-acceptance; an inability to forgive; and, most noteworthy, a pessimistic attitude. Pessimism is important because, being associated with a loss of faith in a positive outcome, it is one of the foundational stones that supports chronic (7) poor health.

Glaucoma (28/1)

Glaucoma indicates a passive-aggressive (28) behavior pattern that does not want to "see" or deal with changes affecting the self (1). Someone exhibiting this behavior pattern might not say no to something he doesn't want to do, but will drag his feet until others give up on the change or move on.

Goiter (38/11/2)

This individual knows (11) what needs to be communicated (3) but does not feel powerful enough (8) to say it (2). The sentiment gets lodged in the throat (28/1). A deficiency of iodine (38/11/2) is also associated with causing goiters.

See also Thyroid Problems.

Gout (18/9)

Gout can be caused by suppressed frustration or anger (8) over issues concerning the self (1). There is a perception that these individuals have not been thanked, recognized, appreciated, or loved for their sacrifices or inputs (9). Gout can also be caused by a pattern of control (9)—a need to make certain that everything is running according to plan. This may be connected to a need to be a savior. Feelings (9) will be hurt when others are not sufficiently appreciative of these individuals' efforts. Gout can also emerge as a result of the misuse of power (8) for personal (1) reasons.

H

Illnesses and diseases beginning with the letter *H* have anger, frustration, power issues, or a need for personal recognition as one of their basic causes.

Halitosis (40/4)

Halitosis is the odor of a rotting foundation (4), fouled by unexpressed emotions or feelings. The *ha* combination, totaling 9, can indicate a desire to withdraw from the world. Odor may be produced to keep others away.

Headache (35/8)

The first three letters of headache, *hea,* numerically transpose to 8, 5, 1. A quick interpretation would be that anger or frustration (8) sufficient to impact the nervous system (5) has a direct influence on the self (1). The *h* and *ea* can be added together for a sum of 5 and subtracted for a remainder of 2. This 5/2 combination can indicate inflexibility or a refusal to cooperate with others, as well as difficulty dealing with changes.

The 35/8 reinforces these themes. The 5 involves issues of flexibility and change. The 3 represents a need to communicate emotions in interpersonal relationships. The 8 indicates an individual who can either be bombastic and aggressive in expressing emotions or be extremely passive and frustrated out of the belief that no one is listening.

Heart (25/7) Disease (26/8) = (51/6)

The combination of 51/6 shows the self (1) being inflexible (5) due to unrealistic expectations (6). Individuals with heart disease may give up a sense of self (1) in order to serve others (2). It's a pattern of not wanting to burden anyone with their feelings and emotions out of fear that they will bother or anger someone and risk being abandoned. The two 6s in the equation reveal the tendency toward unrealistic expectations, which causes constant heartache (6). The number 6 can also bring forth energy of the cosmic mom or dad who feels a need to be there for everyone . . . all of the time (7). Here, the 8 of *disease* is about being locked in anger and frustration related to associations (6) with others (2). Martyrdom reduces to a 2 even though it is part of a negative 6 behavior pattern. There are two 2s in the heart disease equation, which ultimately gives us a sum of 6, indicating the strong presence of martyrdom in the patterns associated with heart disease.

▪ **Congestive (47/11/2) Heart (25/7) Failure (36/9) = (108/9):** There is a strong need to be needed (7) and to control things (4) so that they come out "right" for everyone (7 and 11). This is coupled with feelings of being a failure (9), filling the heart with woe. The 6 indicates that these individuals may have an overwhelming feeling of not having fulfilled their responsibilities and failing those who were counting on them.

The 108/9 total indicates that individuals with congestive heart failure have bottled emotions (9) and frustration (8) over the perception that Spirit (0) hasn't supported them the way they think they should be supported (1).

▪ **Heart (25/7) Attack (11/2) = (36/9):** Individuals who suffer from a heart attack have struggled with not being able to get others (11/2) to do what they believe is best for them (7). The 25 indicates rigidity when interacting with others and the 7 reinforces the control issue of constantly doing for others but having difficulty accepting assistance. The 7 also indicates that trusting others to uphold their end is an issue. Fear and anxiety are being internalized, forcing the heart to pump clumps of negative energy. Eventually, the heart becomes clogged, the energy backs up, and the hoses of the pump rupture.

The 36/9 total indicates difficulty with self-acceptance (3) and a tendency to take on too much responsibility (6) and then be disappointed when the expected thanks, recognition, appreciation, or love

1	2	3	4	5	6	7	8	9
A	B	C	D	E	F	G	H	I
J	K	L	M	N	O	P	Q	R
S	T	U	V	W	X	Y	Z

Heart Disease • Hemorrhoids (Spiritual) **109**

does not materialize. The 9 indicates that too many emotions have been stored in the heart and that the only way to eliminate the excess emotions is by "blowing a gasket."

Heartburn (44/8): *See* Acid Reflux.

Heart (25/7) Cramps (25/7) = (50/5): Heart cramps occur when the pain felt is so great that the individual cannot cry or breathe or express feelings, causing the heart to constrict or cramp. Each time a heart cramp is experienced, the heart muscle is weakened. The underlying issues are lack of timely communication (2); rigidity of attitude (5); and a need to control (7) the environment, whether it's within the family, relationships, or at work. The 7 of the word *cramps* indicates holding on and the sum of 5 signifies not moving forward. The tendency to not ask for help from Spirit is related to the 0.

Hemorrhoids (69/15/6)

The numbers for this condition indicate a pattern of unrealistic expectations (6), ego-related motives (9), and lack of movement (5) due to indecisiveness (1), culminating in a need to force the issue at hand. The challenge for this individual is to stop trying to do what he is not ready to do.

If 4 appears as a major challenge number in an individual's chart, it can increase the probability of hemorrhoids, as this individual has a tendency to procrastinate, struggle to maintain control, and display constrictive behavior patterns.

Spiritual (43/7) Hemorrhoids (69/6) = (112/4): The manifestation of hemorrhoids can also be directly related to one's spiritual journey. In this case, the individual has asked Spirit for an acceleration in spiritual growth or opportunities to fulfill his spiritual mission, or he has told Spirit he is ready to move forward but then refuses, denies, or procrastinates due to a lack of confidence. So, what happens to the energy downloaded from

Spirit? It's trapped and begins seeking a way out. Within three days of denying a commitment to Spirit, hemorrhoids can reach the size of walnuts. Before scheduling surgery to relieve the pain, a person in this situation should try the following: He should apologize to Spirit. In prayer, he should say that he thought he was ready but he's not. He hasn't the courage or trust that he'll be supported. Within four days, the hemorrhoids will shrink and possibly disappear. (It worked for me.)

Hepatitis (44/8)

Adding and subtracting the *h* (8) and *e* (5) of *hepatitis* creates a 4/3. This 4/3 combination can indicate a pattern of stubbornness or procrastination due to underlying feelings of insecurity or inadequacy. These feelings prevent individuals from accepting their personal power (8) without first being validated by others. Other issues related to the 8 are concerns over money; status; social recognition; and the use, nonuse, or abuse of personal power.

The 44 relates to not being grounded (4) on the physical plane (4) and therefore being unable to make the many life-altering decisions required for a proactive life.

- **Hepatitis A (45/9):** Hepatitis A signifies that stubbornness (4) and rigidity (5) have prevented the release of emotional wastes (9).

- **Hepatitis B (46/10/1):** With hepatitis B, there is a need for control (4) and a need for love (6), which can cause individuals with low self-esteem (1) to behave irresponsibly (6).

- **Hepatitis C (47/11/2):** Those with hepatitis C have a bit of a messianic complex (47), which causes them to feel personally responsible for fixing things for everyone, so that everything works the way it's "supposed to" (11) (according to their own view of reality). These individuals also have difficulty letting go of emotional attachments (2), which can lead to chronic (7) hepatitis.

Hernia (37/1)

Hernias are caused by pushing (7) to make something happen due to concern about being judged to be less than what the individual (1) perceives himself to be (7). The 3 indicates feelings of inadequacy and inability to express personal (1) feelings. The *a* as the final letter indicates that the situation could have been avoided if the person had only trusted his inner self (1).

Herpes (35/8) Simplex (35/8) I (I) = (71/8)

Herpes is caused by a virus (8) and viruses are agents for change. The question to be asked is: "What is preventing me from stepping into my power or speaking my truth?"

The 71/8 total involves issues of self-empowerment, frustration, anger, finances, status, and recognition. The 1 is about a lack of confidence (manifesting in patterns of codependency or control) and the 7 represents abandonment issues that can manifest as a fever blister (see below.) The one (1) of *simplex I* (1) indicates that this state has been brought on by the self's (1) insecurities and concerns (7) as they relate to others.

■ **Fever (29/2) Blister (32/5) = (61/7):** The issue associated with a fever blister is difficulty interacting with (2) and/or communicating feelings (9) to others (2).

The 61/7 total represents low self-esteem (1), unrealistic expectations of what "ought to be" in relationships (6), and holding on to feelings and emotions. There is a fear that if emotions are expressed, the individual might be abandoned by those she loves (7). The eruption of the cold sore (37/1) or fever blister (61/7) is the physical manifestation of suppressed feelings of inadequacy and is also related to inadequate communication (3) associated with abandonment (7) issues.

Herpes (35/8) Simplex (35/8) II (2) = (72/9)

The II (2) in Herpes Simplex II indicates this state always involves an *other*.

The two 35/8s may be interpreted two ways: First, excessive appetites (5) fed by feelings of inadequacy (3) may cause individuals to try to dominate or seduce others (8). The second interpretation involves scattered emotions (3), a roller-coaster approach to life (5), and avoiding personal empowerment (8), which all lead to seeking conquests over others to feel empowered.

The 72/9 total indicates that the underlying catalysts for this condition are a need to have another in one's life (2) because of strong abandonment issues (7) and not wanting to be alone. The 9 indicates potential egocentric behavior patterns related to a need to be loved, thanked, or appreciated or to maintain control so as not to be abandoned.

The usual catalyst for a sexually transmitted disease (9) is a lack of self-esteem when dealing with others in relationships/partnerships (2).

See also Sexually Transmitted Diseases.

Hip (24/6) Problems (37/1) = (61/7)

The questions to ask are: "Is there a desire to control (4) what happens to others (2)?" "Are there unrealistic expectations of self and/or others (6) due to abandonment issues?"

If it is the left (16/7) hip (24/6) = (40/4) that is affected, the individual feels responsible for the welfare of others (left = 7) and eventually loses the *flexibility* of personal choice.

If problems occur with the right (35/8) hip (24/6) = (59/14/5), there has been a holding back or not wanting to move forward out of concern over leaving others behind (hip problems = 7). There is a tendency to be excessively rigid (14/5) due to self-esteem issues derived from unrealistic expectations of self and others (6).

The total of 61/7 indicates that the catalysts for hip problems are low self-esteem (1) and a tendency to "carry" others by taking on their

1	2	3	4	5	6	7	8	9
A	B	C	D	E	F	G	H	I
J	K	L	M	N	O	P	Q	R
S	T	U	V	W	X	Y	Z	

Hives • Human Papillomavirus Infection   113

responsibilities (6). The image I see associated with the numeric energy of hip problems is similar to someone carrying a child on her hip. The carrier "throws" out the hip as a ledge to be sat upon. The 7 total reveals an underlying pattern of needing to do for others but not letting others reciprocate due to abandonment issues.

Hives (27/9)

Hives are a manifestation of trying to control or suppress emotions (9) involving others (2). There is anxiety about revealing true feelings, because that may result in being abandoned or rejected (7) by others. The emotions or feelings that have been suppressed become so strong that they push their way to the surface. Each red spot is a raw emotion that hasn't been expressed.

See also Allergy.

Human (21/3) Papillomavirus (67/13/4) Infection (50/5) = (138/12/3)

From right to left, the total of 138/12/3 reveals the following issues: low self-esteem (1), feelings of inadequacy (3), issues with personal power (8), placing others ahead of oneself (1), oversensitivity (2), and avoiding emotional intimacy (3).

Current research has revealed over 120 types of papillomavirus. Researchers believe that at least two types—type 16 and type 18—can cause cancer. I find this very interesting because 16 (1 + 6 = 7) is a karmic number associated with issues of control, abandonment, martyrdom, self-esteem, self-righteousness, and unrealistic expectations of self and others. Type 18 (1 + 8 = 9) may indicate issues revolving around the use or abuse of personal power, timidity or arrogance, and a need to be loved or to maintain control of situations. If you look at the single-digit sums for cervical (1) and cancer (8), the total is also 9.

The numbers for *human* are 21/3 and the last three digits of *human papillomavirus infection* are 12/3. The positive (human) 21/3 is centered, confident, has purpose or direction, and can be an innovator (all related to a positive 1). The individual under the influence of this energy can also be tactful, diplomatic, a mediator with good communication skills (positive 2 characteristics), and have balanced both feminine (2) and masculine (1) energies to become productive, creative, joyful, socially interactive, and visionary (positive 3.) The negative 12/3 may be either too timid or too arrogant (negative 1) or overly sensitive or insensitive (negative 2). The negative 3 total can indicate someone who is emotionally closed, socially withdrawn (projecting a facade of social engagement), scattered, has a tendency to exaggerate (to increase social status), has feelings of inadequacy, and can be unforgiving toward those she feels have "let her down" or don't appreciate her sacrifices.

See also Cervical Cancer *and* Sexually Transmitted Disease.

Hypertension (69/15/6)

With 6s at either end of the equation, the main issue with hypertension involves unrealistic expectations. The 9 indicates emotions related to a need to maintain control and to do it "my way." This is reinforced by the appearance of the 5, which, in this case, indicates rigidity and lack of movement or release. If the negative emotions associated with these tendencies cannot be released, they can become poisonous to the entire system, leading to all sorts of complications.

The *hy* of *hypertension* has a sum of 6. Subtracting the *y* from the *h* gives a total of 1. This 6/1 combination indicates that feeling obligations to others, this individual will assume too much responsibility. There is also a need to advise and counsel others and to be validated (1) for the counseling (6). If these patterns cannot be modified to avoid frustration, they will eventually affect the heart, which is the seat of surrender and allowing.

As an aside, the 69 indicates difficulty balancing the male/female aspects of the self. This can be another cause of unbalanced emotions associated with hypertension.

See also under Blood Pressure.

Hypoglycemia (67/13/4)

The main issue associated with hypoglycemia is an inability to make transitions (13/4). The difficulty stems from self-imposed feelings of inadequacy (3), low self-esteem (1), and control issues (4). The 67 reinforces these themes. The 7, like the 4, is associated with control issues. It also indicates a form of paralysis, either mental or emotional, due to an inability to make a decision. With hypoglycemia, the mental/emotional processes consume a great deal of energy very rapidly and, as a result, the body reacts by calling for more energy—ASAP!

I

Illnesses and diseases beginning with the letter I involve intense emotions concerning the self.

Impotence (46/1)

Low self-esteem (1) leads to a need to be in control (4) and to be loved (6). The control issue is directly linked with anxieties concerning unrealistic expectations of the self (1) and/or others (6). There is a fear that if these expectations are not met, the result will be rejection or abandonment.

Indigestion (62/8)

Indigestion manifests after either expressed anger or suppressed frustration (8), which can lead to sensitivity and communication issues (2) in interpersonal communications (2) within close relationships (6).

Influenza (45/9)

Influenza is caused by a virus (9); viruses are always agents for change (5). The 5, of the 45, calls for having a sufficient amount of self-confidence and flexibility to deal with life's capriciousness. The 4 indicates a bit of procrastination, and/or stubbornness (4) associated with express-ing emotions and feelings (9). Symptoms associated with influenza—inflammation of the respiratory tract (7), fever, chills, and muscular pain—are physical manifestations of hidden or suppressed emotions and feelings (9). In extreme cases, a failure to express these inner feelings (9) can initiate a shutdown of our life support systems. As agents for change (1), one of the functions performed by viruses is to terminate life-forms that cannot change and become stronger from the experience.

The negative 9 total can also indicate a pattern of interactions with others based on a need to be loved or to maintain control of a relation-ship (or population); this pattern is directly linked with abandonment issues.

See also Cold *and* Flu.

Ingrown (46/1) Toenail (31/4) = (77/14/5)

Fear (7) and anxiety (7) lead the self (1) to hesitate (4) when it comes to dealing with movement (5).

If the ingrown toenail is on the left foot, the nail curls because the individual feels overwhelmed by incoming energies. If the ingrown toe-nail is on the right foot, there is hesitation about moving forward and this restriction of the forward flow of one's own energy causes the toe-nail to curl back on itself.

Insomnia (40/4)

The cause of insomnia is linked with a belief that there isn't going to be enough time to do everything that needs to be done for everyone else, which will lead others to become angry or be disappointed. This per-ceived failure to meet self-imposed expectations stirs up abandonment anxieties. Lack of control over one's life is also an issue. Artificially imposed deadlines and micromanagement stemming from these emo-tional issues are the catalysts for insomnia.

J

Illnesses and diseases beginning with the letter *J* involve issues of doing for self and having confidence.

Joint (23/5) Problems (37/1) = (60/6)

The overriding issue associated with joints is movement (5). Joints are transfer points for energy. Joint problems indicate that the individual (1) feels a need to prove himself (37). This belief puts an undue strain on the individual and makes him feels responsible (6) for the welfare of others. The 0 indicates that he is not listening to his higher self.

If the joint problem is on the left side of the body, the person is reacting to incoming responsibilities. If the joint problem is on the right side of the body, he is reacting to what is perceived as a need to prove himself (6).

■ **Joint Pain (45/9):** The cause of joint pain is a failure to release emotions (9) due to patterns of stubbornness (5), being overly amenable (5), or having a need to be in control (4).

To help alleviate joint pain, visualize energy either flowing toward the joint or away from the joint. Next, visualize everything that transports energy (from capillaries to nerves, muscles, tendons, and cartilage) expanding to allow more energy to pass through in a shorter period of time.

See also Arthritis, *as the same patterns apply.*

K

Illnesses and diseases beginning with the letter *K* involve issues of sensitivity and needing to do what is "right" for others.

Kidney (32/5) Problems (37/1) = (69/15/6)

Kidney problems are the result of not being able to deal with changes (5). Poor communication skills, hypersensitivity to the feelings of others (2), and/or a desire to withdraw from social interactions (3) could be the root causes. The function of the kidneys is to release the wastes of the body, mind, and spirit. If these wastes are not released, they back up and can poison the entire body.

The combination of 69/15/6 contains the 5 of *kidney* and the 1 of *problems*. It indicates patterns of rigidity (5) related to low self-esteem (1) and a need to be loved or to maintain control (9). This individual may become a *doer* or *controller* within relationships (6).

Knuckle (23/5) Cracking (39/3) = (62/8)

"Woe is me! What can I do?" Chronic knuckle cracking indicates feelings of never being able to live up to one's own or others' expectations (6). Other common sentiments include: "What are they (2) thinking?" "I'm afraid to be me (8)." "I'm frustrated (8)." "I'm bored (26/8)."

```
1 2 3 4 5 6 7 8 9
A B C D E F G H I
J K L M N O P Q R
S T U V W X Y Z
```
Laryngitis • Lung (Emphysema) 119

> ## L
> Illnesses and diseases beginning with the letter *L* involve communication issues and feelings of inadequacy.

Laryngitis (53/8)

In laryngitis, the voice becomes rigid (5) when feelings of inadequacy and a need for acceptance (3) trigger issues involving anger, frustration, personal power, money, status, and recognition (8).

Lung (18/9)

There are three basic breathing patterns: The first is a relaxed pattern of inhalation and exhalation. In this state, negative emotions can be brought forth, processed, and then expelled from the body. The second is a rapid and shallow breathing pattern that occurs whenever anxiety or fear is experienced. The shallowness of the breath does not supply enough energy to expel negative emotions (9) from the lung, so some remain. The third pattern is one of not breathing. When we cease to breathe, the usual cause is a "heart cramp" or fear. Heart cramps are caused by the ego not wanting to deal with the pain of the moment and locking it away in the heart. The only way to ease this cramping is to breathe through the pain; otherwise, the pain is locked in the heart and emotions are locked in the lungs.

A self-imposed suppression of individual (1) power (8) and emotional expression (9) becomes the catalyst for lung-related health issues. Notice that each ailment listed below has a 4 as part of the numeric composition, indicating issues revolving around control, holding on, and procrastination.

■ **Emphysema (42/6):** Emphysema is usually the result of long-term behavior patterns that have as their core issues cooperation with (2) or control of others (4) and a failure to take personal responsibility (6).

1	2	3	4	5	6	7	8	9
A	B	C	D	E	F	G	H	I
J	K	L	M	N	O	P	Q	R
S	T	U	V	W	X	Y	Z	

120   Lung (Pleurisy) • Lupus Erythematosis

■ **Pleurisy (44/8):** The underlying cause is suppressed (44) anger, irritation, and stubbornness, or a reactionary personality coupled with the frustration of being told what to do and when by distant and impersonal authorities (8). Under the surface is a need for recognition and appreciation for good deeds; when that recognition fails to materialize, the individual can become angry, irritated, or passive-aggressive (all associated with the number 8).

■ **Pneumonia (45/9):** When it comes to expressing emotions (9), there is a tendency to procrastinate (4) or be too rigid in attitude (5) to express them. As a result, they remain in the lung (9), eventually materializing as a liquid (9).

■ **Tuberculosis (47/11/2):** The 47/11/2 combination indicates individuals with a heightened sensitivity (7) who need to make (4) things happen a certain way—that is, the way they think it should happen (11). The 11, the first master number, allows people to see "above the clouds"—the way it "could be." However, it does not always give them the opportunity or the power to implement this vision of the way it ought to be. This causes a tendency to hold back emotions or not speak up. It can also cause the opposite reaction: hitting people between the eyes with the baseball bat of perceived truths. In either case, the core issue will always come back to how openly these individuals interact with others (2).

Sufferers of tuberculosis can be inflexible and resistant to change (4). Change is "good" if they control it; change is "bad" if they can't control it. Involuntary change pushes their abandonment buttons (7). With tuberculosis, there is no wind left in the lungs to speak the message (11); all available space has been taken up by suppressed emotions.

Lupus (17/8) Erythematosis (54/9) = (71/8)

"As with other autoimmune diseases, the exact cause, or trigger, for lupus remains unknown. Research has shown that the disease results when a specific set of susceptible genes [64/1] is exposed to a combination of environmental factors [91/1] such as infectious agents [70/7], certain drugs such as anticonvulsants [51/6], some penicillins [59/5], and estrogen therapy [79/7], excessive ultraviolet light [115/7], physical trauma [59/5], or emotional stress [60/6]. It is not known which of these factors sets the illness in motion."*

Notice that the single-digit numbers (1, 5, 6, and 7) placed next to the possible medical causes of lupus when added together reduce to the number 1. For me, this indicates that the initial trigger starts with behavior patterns that are directed at pleasing others and not the self (1) or pleasing oneself and not others.

Self-esteem issues (1) coupled with anxieties (7) about stepping into or using personal power (8) are the catalysts that initiate lupus. Because of the presence of anxiety (7), these individuals try to control (4) their physical environment (5) by acting either to be loved or to maintain control of relationships (9). The amount of energy exerted to maintain this state exhausts both the etheric and physical bodies, causing a systemwide breakdown.

Lupus is a 17/8 and the total for lupus erythematosis is 71/8. This shows that a lack of confidence leads to a pattern of being either too timid or too aggressive (1) in interactions with others. This either-or pattern is influenced by the negative 7 and the need either to be loved, thanked, and appreciated or to control all aspects of a situation to guarantee a "successful" outcome. Other aspects of negative 7 energy are impatience and fears of abandonment. These individuals' abandonment anxieties are fed by feelings that others will perceive them as being less capable than they see themselves and will cast them from the group. People under the influence of the negative 7 also have a need to do for others but find it very difficult to let others do for them. It's a trust issue. The 8 total can indicate issues concerning money, authority, self-empowerment, status, and recognition. It can also indicate suppressed anger and frustration or anger and frustration that are hard to control.

---

*Encarta Online Encyclopedia, s.v. "Lupus Erythematosus," http://Encarta.msn.com (accessed August 20, 2008).

```
          1 2  3 4 5 6 7 8 9
          A B  C D E F G H I
          J K  L M N O P Q R
          S T  U V W X Y Z
```

122   Lupus Erythematosis (Systemic) • Lyme Disease

▪ **Systemic (32/5) Lupus (17/8) Erythematosis (54/9) = (103/4):** The 103/4 total of the more complete name of this disease says that control issues (4) fueled by low self-esteem (1) and a feeling of disconnectedness from spirit (0), along with feelings of inadequacy and scatteredness (3), lead to stubbornness and apprehension about moving forward.

This pattern can be further supported by interpreting the *sys* of the word *systemic* (systemwide): The letter *s* as the first letter in a word or name indicates one who is seldom satisfied with the status quo (1). This person wants things to change, but she wants the changes to match her perception of what ought to be. The *y* indicates an analytical personality and feeds into fears of making mistakes or being embarrassed by making the "wrong" choice (according to others). The indecisiveness of the negative *y* (7) energy can result in mental, emotional, or physical paralysis. As part of this pattern, those individuals who are susceptible to this illness will mentally prepare at least five options, four backup choices, three crisis plans, two emergency strategies, and a worst-case scenario. At the last moment, all plans are ignored or forgotten. Faith in a positive outcome begins to wane, and anxiety and apprehension come to the forefront. The second *s* makes this individual realize that she is still dissatisfied and that the only way to break the pattern is to "let go and let God." Stop trying to make things happen and learn to allow them to happen at a divine level.

Lyme (19/1) Disease (26/8) = (45/9)

This is an infectious bacterial disease (110/2) triggered by the bite of a tick. Numerically, the word *tick* transposes to 16/7, a number that signals it is time for self-examination, time to stop trying to save (or control) the world. The 110/2 indicates the possibility that this individual is tired of doing for others and desires some reciprocal attention. The primary issues that activate the events leading to this disease are low self-esteem (1) and a tendency to internalize emotions (9).

The 19/1 of *Lyme* indicates a personality that can swing between being Mother Teresa, if things are going well, and Genghis Khan, if they're not. This is reinforced through the 45/9 combination. Both 4 and 5 are numbers associated with issues of control and rigidity. The 4 represents behavior patterns associated with control, procrastination, stubbornness, and being overly logical. The 5 represents patterns that can swing between rigidity and hyperflexibility in interactions with others. Whenever 9 appears, the core issue is: Are you doing what you love or are you acting to be loved or to maintain control? This illness has a greater impact on the *doer* personality type than it does on those identified as *clingers* or *controllers*.

One of the first symptoms of Lyme disease is a rash (19/1). The purpose of the rash is to see if we are paying attention to ourself (1). If we are, we seek treatment. If not, the disease progresses as repressed or suppressed emotional feelings (9) and begins to sap the energy of the immune system (*see also* Autoimmune Disorder). Other symptoms are:

▪ **Fever (29/2):** Fever is the body's way of burning off excess emotional clutter (29).

▪ **Headache (35/8):** Headache results from an imbalance (5) caused by feelings of inadequacy and apprehension (3) associated with personal empowerment, status, finances, and recognition (8).

▪ **Joint (23/5) Pain (22/4) = (45/9):** Our joints support us and are responsible for movement. Painful joints signal we are not releasing or moving energy. Joints on the left side of the body process incoming energy. The joints on the right side of the body assist in the release of energy and intentions. Ultimately, joint pain is a direct result of rigid (5) and controlling (4) behaviors when dealing with others (9).

▪ **Muscle (19/1) Pain (22/4) = (41/5):** Pain (4) is always a signal to pay attention to foundational issues. A 5 calls for flexibility and balance. Individuals (1) afflicted with muscle pain can be very inflexible, even rigid or stubborn (4), when it comes to change (5). The opposite can also be true: fearing abandonment, some individuals become overly flexible "doers," doing for others even when they don't feel like it. Friction (5) is generated within the muscles by patterns of behavior that swing between being a Mother Theresa and a Genghis Khan. When things go well, the saint appears. When things aren't going well, the warrior emerges. These erratic transformations can pull and stretch the muscles beyond the norm, thereby causing muscle pain.

▪ **Severe Fatigue (62/8):** Seeing themselves as responsible (6) for others (2), these individuals feel they need to be in charge (8) to make certain that everything is taken care of according to plan . . . their plan. This pattern is quite exhausting.

▪ **Stiff (24/6) Neck (15/6) = (39/3):** Feelings of inadequacy (3), alleviated by nurturing others (6), lead to a control pattern. These individuals will do for others but find it difficult to allow others to do for them (9). This can make them "stiff-necked."

If Lyme disease is not diagnosed in time, arthritis (5) can develop. *See* Arthritis; *see also* Stiff Neck *under* Neck.

M

Illnesses and diseases beginning with the letter M involve patterns of manipulation and foundational issues.

Macular (24/6) Degeneration (63/9) = (87/15/6)

The 87/15/6 signifies a behavior pattern that includes unrealistic expectations for self and/or others (6), difficulty with change (5), self-esteem issues (1), anxieties about abandonment (7), and difficulty dealing with personal power (8).

The issues associated with the 24/6 involve assuming too much or too little responsibility (6), a need for control (4), and sensitivity (2).

The 63/9 represents a need to run other people's lives (6), and feelings of inadequacy or self-acceptance (3). There is also a desire to be thanked, recognized, appreciated, or loved for sacrifices made (9) or to be able to maintain control of social interactions (9). The *de* indicates behaviors associated with degenerative patterns that reinforce the need to be loved or to maintain control (9) to sustain a sense of self-worth.

Macular degeneration comes from not wanting to see the reality of lifelong behavior patterns or to look at the results of a lifetime of (perceived) disappointments (7) or ineffectualness (8). These individuals allow their ability to process light waves to wither and eventually die. Living in the darkness, they no longer have to look at anything.

Mononucleosis (57/12/3) / also called Glandular Fever (65/11/2)

Mononucleosis is initiated by the Epstein-Barr (55/1) virus (see below). As mentioned earlier, viruses are agents of change. The issues associated with this virus and illness revolve around fighting to hold back change (55) due to poor self-esteem (1) or trying to change the way others think or do things (55) and feeling thwarted (11/2). In either case, the physical body becomes exhausted.

The 57/12/3 shows that those afflicted with this illness are very sensitive people. Outwardly, they may appear very social (3) but beneath that facade is a concern as to how they are perceived by others (2). If they do not have a strong sense of self (1), they may suffer from low self-esteem (1), which can weaken the immune system. The number 7 indicates not wanting to be embarrassed or humiliated (and thus abandoned). The 5 intimates a desire for freedom or change but is neutralized by the anxiety of the 7.

These individuals can be empathic (3) and it may be possible for them to absorb their partner's emotional history (2) either by being in his or her physical presence or by kissing (7). Absorbing someone else's emotional history can be very exhausting (2)! The exhaustion (1) can be caused by stress (1) related to being hypersensitive to the emotions and feelings of others (2) and not always having the courage (7) to speak up (3) or take action (5). The physical symptoms of mononucleosis— fatigue, fever, sore throat, and nausea—are related to the body trying to rid itself of excess negative emotions (7).

The first consonant/vowel combination, *mo,* indicates either a tendency toward codependency or an attempt at total independence to avoid any type of dependency.

The 65/11/2 total of *glandular fever* indicates a tendency to spread oneself too thin, trying to do too much for too many (2) with insufficient energy, resources, or opportunities (11). This can lead to a rigid attitude (5) and feelings of martyrdom (6).

Mononucleosis is often shortened to *mono,* which also reduces to the number 3.

Epstein-Barr (55/1) Virus (26/8) = (81/9): As mentioned above, a core issue revealed by these numbers is the tendency to fight to hold back changes (55) due to poor self-esteem (1).

The 81/9 indicates two possible behavior patterns, both motivated by fear of abandonment: individuals either misuse personal (1) power (8) to maintain control within relationships (9) or they sacrifice the self (1) and personal power (8) to sustain relationships (9). The amount of energy required to sustain either behavior pattern is, literally, exhausting (47/2).

Multiple (36/9) Chemical (36/9) Sensitivities (53/8) = (125/8)

The underlying catalyst for this health issue is a history of not releasing emotions (9) or expressing feelings (3) because of a need to be loved or to maintain control (9) within relationships (6). There is also a desire to do what is "right" (9). However, self-imposed feelings of inadequacy (3), apprehension over the consequences of accepting and using personal power (8), hypersensitivity to the environment or others (2), and difficulty with personal (1) interactions prevent these individuals from breaking patterns of codependency or putting others first (2, 6, and 9).

Karma associated with the number 8 reveals that these individuals (1) have an aversion to the world of business and commerce (8) because of a fear of failure or humiliation. They may have cellular memories of past negative patterns of leadership (8) that caused hardships for others (2). The dual 9s represent unreleased feelings or emotions that can be the catalyst for war between the body and its environment. It is as though these individuals are caught between wanting to withdraw from the world (3) and wanting to be in charge (8) of it.

In the 125/8 total, we see an unheeded desire for movement and change (5) influenced by issues involving codependency, difficulty releasing emotional and sentimental attachments, timely communication, and negative or frustrating interactions with others (all related to the number 2). A diminished sense of self (1) inhibits a full exploration of personal empowerment (8). Another potential pattern is a tendency to put self (1) after others (2). This can make individuals overly amenable (5) when trying to make others happy and generate underlying feelings of frustration or anger (8) with oneself or others. This pattern can lead to a desire to withdraw from the world. Developing adverse reactions to their physical environment allows these individuals to withdraw from society without having to hurt anyone's feelings.

See also Autoimmune Disorder.

Multiple (36/9) Sclerosis (38/11/2) = (74/11/2) (MS = 5)

Notice the frequency with which the numbers 2, 3, 6, 7, 9, and 11 occur throughout the symptoms and terms associated with this disease, as outlined in this section. Also, notice that MS equals 5, a number that deals with physical movement.

Multiple sclerosis is a chronic (7) disease affecting the foundation (4) of the central nervous system (9). It destroys (8) tissues of the brain (8) and spinal cord (3). The 9 indicates a pattern of not releasing emotions or expressing personal feelings because of a need to be loved or to maintain control (9) within relationships/partnerships/commitments (6). This pattern stems from self-imposed feelings of inadequacy (3).

The 38/11/2 of *sclerosis* reinforces this pattern. The negative 3 again raises issues of self-confidence and self-acceptance. The 8 relates to being anxious or fearful about using personal power. The 11 indicates that, either cognitively or intuitively, these individuals can see "the big picture," but don't think they can get others to understand or see it. This can result in suppressing frustration and/or anger (8) so as not to hurt or agitate others (2). The rationale is, "If I hurt or agitate others, they may abandon me." (This pattern of thought is related to the number 7, which appears in the sum.) In this instance, 2 represents a hypersensitive receptivity to energetic feedback from others that overloads the nervous system (8).

It's thought that there might be a genetic predisposition for contracting MS. I believe that the "predisposition" is activated by familial personalities and behavior patterns that are repeated through generations. (It's the same with heart disease, diabetes, and any other genetic condition.) The genetic trigger cannot be fired without sufficient tension placed on it. The tension is the suppressed frustration or anger generated by knowing what needs to be done but being unable to do it because of indifference, hostility, or a lack of cooperation from others.

The following descriptive terms and symptoms of MS all have numbers that relate to the 74/11/2 combination. This combination indicates a need to control (4) events as they unfold—so as not to be blamed or abandoned if something should go wrong (7). There's a feeling of being personally responsible for everyone's welfare (11) and, as a result, there is a want/desire/need for cooperation and partnership (2) to carry out the "mission." If these individuals don't get the cooperation or understanding they feel they need, their energy field begins to contract. This "contraction" will eventually affect the nervous system like an electrical blackout spreading through a power grid, forcing the grid to shut down.

■ **Central (28/1) Nervous (33/6) System (20/2) = (81/9) (CNS = 9):**
These numbers indicate a tendency toward being passive-aggressive (28),
a martyr (33), and hypersensitive (20). The 81/9 total is a consolidation
of these negative energies. The negative 1 relates to poor self-esteem. The
8 represents power issues: who has it? The 9 deals directly with unexpressed emotions and feelings that become trapped in a continuous loop
through the CNS, creating friction.

■ **Chronic (43/7) Degenerative (61/7) Disease (26/8) = (130/4):** The
number 13 calls for making transitions in life. Those under the influence
of the negative 13 are fearful of letting go, not knowing what the future
will hold, and find it very difficult to "hear" their higher self (0). The 4
indicates a pattern of being stubborn, reactionary, procrastinating, and/
or controlling. The words *chronic* and *degenerative* both carry negative 7
energy, indicating a pattern of withdrawal.

■ **Destruction (49/13/4) of (12/3) Myelin (33/6) = (94/13/4):** Failure
to move forward (13) in life and let go (9) of fears and anxieties causes the
process of creation (3) to slow down or cease to function. The destruction of myelin is known as *demyelination* (65/11/2). What destroys the
myelin is friction (49/13/4)—a push/pull energy generated by indecision
(56/11/2) and control issues. Notice that the 56 of *indecision* and the 65
of *demyelination* both reduce to 11, then 2, the same combination as *multiple sclerosis.*

■ **Loss (11/2) of (12/3) Coordination (65/11/2) = (88/16/7):** This particular symptom is the universe saying STOP! The 16 is a karmic number, indicating a messianic behavior pattern—a need to make certain that
everyone and everything is perfect so as not to be blamed for the mistakes
of others. The loss of coordination says, "Stop trying to coordinate everything; it's too much for one person." The 7 calls for overcoming abandonment issues and having more faith and patience (with oneself as well as
with others). It also calls for letting go, which means letting others pick

up some of the slack. The 88 is about personal power . . . use it or lose it, but don't abuse it. Again the 11s appear, indicating the ability to see the way it ought to be, but not necessarily having the power, influence, or opportunity to make it so.

■ **Muscular (27/9) Weakness (25/7) = (52/7):** Notice the frequency with which the 2, 5, and 7 appear. The underlying catalyst for muscular weakness is a pattern of oversensitivity bordering on empathic (2), a need to be needed or useful (7), and a tendency to overextend oneself (5).

Being rigid (5) with emotions and feelings (9) can put a strain on the muscular system, thus weakening it. The 27/9 reveals a pattern of needing to do for others (2). Because of a concern for correctness—related to the abandonment issues of the number 7—and a feeling that others could be unreliable or untrustworthy, these individuals tend to want to do things their own way.

The 52/7 total indicates that these individuals may feel alone and abandoned and therefore be hesitant to venture into the world. If there is no forward movement, muscles may atrophy. Atrophy transposes to a 4, a number that represents foundations. The muscular system is part of the body's foundation. If we don't support ourself, why should our muscles?

■ **Speech (29/2) Disturbances (45/9) = (74/11/2):** The total of *speech disturbances* is the same combination as that of *multiple sclerosis*. Speech disturbances can be a means of getting others to listen more closely and be more cooperative.

The number 2 involves timely and compassionate communication. The 29, like the 74, reduces to an 11, which represents a core issue of MS: individuals knowing (or thinking they know) what needs to be said or communicated to others but being unable to get the message across. The 29 is a number that brings emotional tests. With this symptom, these tests are likely to involve emotionally letting go of messianic energies (7) that make individuals feel personally responsible for getting "the message" out to everyone. When or if they can't get the message out, the 45/9, indicating stubbornness (4) and rigid emotions (5 and 9), exacerbates this pattern. It's all part of the push/pull energy of wanting things to change and, yet, remain the same.

■ **Visual (21/3) Disturbances (45/9) = (66/12/3):** The number 3 is associated with vision. A negative 3 wants to pull back, hide, or withdraw from the outer world. Physically, those under the influence of the negative 3 may have rounded shoulders, a habit of folding their arms across their chest, and a tendency to look down or not make direct eye contact. In this instance, the 21/3 reveals a pattern of low self-esteem (1), difficulty communicating (2), and feelings of inadequacy (3). Combine this with the 45/9 pattern—indicating being stubborn (4) and somewhat rigid (5) emotionally (9)—and you get someone who has lost optimism (3) and become tired of looking at what cannot be changed (66). The individual comes to feel that there is no need to see more.

Myofascial (41/5) Pain (22/4) Dysfunction (51/6) = (114/6)

The words *myofascial pain* add up to 63/9. The 9 deals with issues of both control and codependency, of doing to be loved or to maintain control and having difficulty releasing things. The 63 indicates several potential behavior patterns that could be the catalyst for the 9 pattern. The 3 can bring feelings of inadequacy and anxiety about communicating feelings. The 6 may represent trying to do too much for too many with too little.

Myofascial, as a 41/5, indicates that some of the underlying issues may be related to low self-esteem, displayed as either timidity or arrogance (1); a tendency toward stubbornness or acquiescence (4); and difficulty dealing with the physical world (5).

The 22/4 of *pain* is a reminder to examine mental, emotional, and physical foundations to locate the excess negative energy that is the catalyst for the pain. Individuals should ask themselves the following questions: Have I looked at my relationships with others (2)? Am I out of balance or concerned about change (5)? Am I being too flexible in meeting the needs of others, without communicating my desires (1, 2, 5, 6)? Is there underlying resentment not being expressed? Am I grinding my teeth because others are not doing what I want them to do (22/4)? Are there control issues (4, 6)?

The numeric total for *dysfunction* is 51/6. The 6 reveals a pattern of unrealistic expectations for the self and/or others (6). It also brings to the surface issues associated with responsibility (taking on too much or too little), self-esteem (1), and the ability to "be in the moment" (5).

The 114/6 total indicates that individuals may be lacking in confidence, not be centered, and have issues with control and responsibility.

N

Illnesses and diseases beginning with the letter N involve emotions and the nervous system.

Nail Biting (52/7)

This indicates a nervousness dealing with others (2), which leads to difficulty with movement (5). Questions surface: "Which way should I go?" "What should I say?" The 7 signifies anxiety about making the "wrong" decision and being humiliated or abandoned as a result.

Neck (15/6) Pain (22/4) = (37/1)

Neck pain indicates flexibility (5) issues involving the self (1) and unrealistic expectations (6). Those experiencing neck pain need to consider what it is that they don't want to turn and look at. The pain (4) serves to call attention to the foundational issues that are the catalysts of this condition.

The 37/1 total reveals an underlying pattern of anxiety about outcomes (7), pessimism and moodiness (3), and a desire to avoid social interactions that may turn out different from expectations.

■ **Stiff (24/6) Neck (15/6) = (39/12/3):** Because both *stiff* and *neck* transpose to the number 6, the main issues involve maintaining unrealistic expectations of the self (1) or others and a stubbornness (4) or rigidity (5) when it comes to interacting with others (2) or doing things differently.

The 3s on either side of the 39/12/3 reveal that feelings of inadequacy are the catalyst for neck stiffness. The 2 indicates difficulty with cooperation or compromise. The 1 points to the self as the center of the equation and the 9 reflects difficulty letting go or changing directions (because this may conflict with being loved or maintaining control of a situation).

Nerves (29/11/2)

The 29 is a number that brings emotional tests into a person's life. Issues concerning the nerves involve knowing the way things ought to be (11) but being unable to make them that way either because of poor communication skills (2), acting as an emotional pincushion for others (9), or being hypersensitive to everyone except oneself. The questions to ask are: Can I let go of emotional attachments? Can I stop trying to make things happen the way I think they should? Can I learn to trust others?

O

Illnesses and diseases beginning with the letter O involve issues of responsibility and relationships.

Obesity (32/5)

Numerically, the *o* transposes to a 6, which represents, among other things, food, sweets, and unrealistic expectations. The letters *o* and

1	2	3	4	5	6	7	8	9
A	B	C	D	E	F	G	H	I
J	K	L	M	N	O	P	Q	R
S	T	U	V	W	X	Y	Z	

134   Ovarian Cysts

b can be added together for a sum of 8 or subtracted for a total of 4. This 8/4 combination indicates individuals who desire to be in charge and do things their way or to be in charge but not be bothered by the details. Alternatively, it could also reflect the opposite pattern—a fear of accepting personal empowerment (8), resulting in procrastination. The 2 of the 32/5 total for *obesity* reflects hypersensitivity, difficulty with partnerships, and codependency (2). The 3 identifies feelings of inadequacy and difficulty with self-acceptance. The negative 5 represents excesses and difficulty with change stemming from low self-esteem.

  See also Weight Problem.

Ovarian (35/8) Cysts (14/5) = (49/13/4)

The core issue is one of power (8). It is about allowing one's power to be constrained (5) by others due to self-imposed feelings of inadequacy (3).

  A lack of self-expression or optimism (3) causes the flow of energy through the area (5) to slow. Negative particles of energy accumulate and form a lump, further constricting the flow. This accumulation of negative energy represents anger and frustration in relation to personal power (8).

  Ovarian cysts also indicate issues regarding making transitions, letting go, and moving on (13). The 4s at either end of the 49/13/4 numeric combination suggest individuals who can be stubborn, clinging, and controlling when it comes to making changes. Feelings of low self-esteem (1) and self-imposed feelings of inadequacy (3) make it difficult for these individuals to express their true feelings or emotions (9).

	P

Illnesses and diseases beginning with the letter *P* involve issues of control and trust.

Parkinson's (46/1) Disease (26/8) = (72/9)

The main issues associated with Parkinson's are unrealistic expectations of self or others (6) and a need to be in control (4) due to problems with self-esteem (1).

The 72/9 indicates hypersensitivity to the actions of others (2) because of personal anxieties about abandonment (7). Those afflicted with Parkinson's disease also have a need to know how others feel about them (9) but do not want, or are unable, to reveal their own feelings (9). The 9 total reveals a pattern of acting in order to be loved by others or trying to control others.

The longer someone tries to maintain this pattern, the more energy has to be funneled through the nervous (7) system (2) so that the physical body can respond to the program being run by the mental body. The entire process eventually overwhelms and exhausts the nervous system, causing it to "misfire." The misfiring of the neurons (7) sends inconsistent and confusing messages to the receptors (2), creating the following symptoms:

- **Bent Head and Spine (69/15/6):** The weight of being a perfectionist (6), along with a sense of undue responsibility for the self or others (6), causes rigidity (5). The shortening of the neck muscles, which causes the bending of the head and spine in a downward direction, indicates a desire to avoid having to look at what cannot be changed or improved upon.

- **Faulty Balance (42/6):** Faulty balance is caused by trying to maintain control (4), attempting to balance (2) everything for everyone so that everyone is happy (6). A good analogy is someone who has her arms so full of packages for others that she can't see over them and, as a result, has difficulty maintaining her balance.

■ **Lack of Facial Expression (98/17/8):** This is caused by not wanting to reveal emotions (9) and/or the suppression of personal (1) anger or frustration (8) toward others.

■ **Muscular Rigidity (83/11/2):** Knowing the way things are "supposed" to be (11) but not having the power (8) or the influence over others (2) to make them that way leads to feelings of inadequacy and failure (3) and manifests as muscular rigidity.

■ **Poor Coordination (93/12/3):** Those experiencing poor coordination have so much going on that they cannot coordinate all of the energies involved. Not centered on themselves (1), they are constantly sensing the energy and emotions (9) of those (2) around them. They scatter (3) their energy and thoughts, trying either to please or to control others (9).

■ **Slow Body Movements (70/7):** In this case, the 7 represents apprehension about moving forward because of anxiety about having to leave people behind. The 7 also indicates uncertainty, which is reflected in slow body movements. It is associated with paralysis, be it mental, emotional, spiritual, or physical.

Pimple (35/8)

Anger, frustration (8), or confusion (3) of the ego concerning issues of change (5) rises to the surface forming a pimple—a blockage of negative emotional energy.

The catalysts for pimples are feelings of inadequacy, an introverted personality (3), and difficulty expressing emotions, especially those dealing with anger or frustration (8). Feelings "boil" to the surface and, if not consciously recognized and released, will fester until they are drained.

See also Boil.

Psoriasis (44/8)

A major underlying cause of psoriasis is suppressed anger and frustration (8) associated with not being able to control (44) or implement personal agendas (8). There are issues over status, recognition, finances, rewards, dealings with authorities (earthly or celestial), personal empowerment, and loyalty (8). The 44 can make individuals defiant, stubborn, overly concerned with minutiae, argumentative, and/or procrastinators. These behaviors are the result of the 44/8 requiring life-altering decisions without prior knowledge of the outcome, alternatives, or consequences.

The itching (7) that accompanies untreated lesions is associated with a desire to move forward while at the same time feeling apprehensive about a successful outcome (due to abandonment issues). If recognition is delayed or not received, anger, irritation, or passive-aggressive behaviors can be the catalysts for new lesions and more itching.

R

Illnesses and diseases beginning with the letter R involve intense emotions concerning the self.

Restlessness (39/3)

The issue is scattered/unfocused energy (3), associated with emotions (9) that need to be acknowledged and dealt with by communicating your feelings to the appropriate party.

S

Illnesses and diseases beginning with the letter S indicate personal dissatisfaction with some current state.

Sciatica (29/11/2)

The main issue associated with sciatica is resisting change, especially change involving emotions. If the condition manifests on the left side, it indicates difficulty dealing with incoming energy. This is usually associated with a perception that the individual needs to take on more responsibility, even though she doesn't want to. If the sciatica affects the right side, there is hesitancy about moving forward in a way that is in the best interest of the higher self (11/2). The problem is the individual doesn't want to leave anyone behind (9) or hurt anyone's feelings (9).

Looking at the 29/11/2 combination, 9 brings hypersensitivity in interactions with others (2). It can also indicate someone who is an emotional pincushion, picking up and holding the emotions of others. The 11, as the first master number, brings the ability to see the way things ought to be but also frustration over not being able to make them that way. The final 2 indicates a need to communicate feelings. The *a* at the end of *sciatica* indicates some "Oh shoot!" moment caused by a failure to honor the self in all relationships. This individual may have taken on the role of codependent or enabler within a relationship.

Seizures (41/5)

The catalyst for seizures is confusion (44/8). The 44/8 indicates having to make a decision about whether or not to step into power (8). It calls for drawing a line and saying, "No more." The confusion can be caused by a lack of confidence (1) and a conscious or unconscious tendency to be stubborn, procrastinate, get lost in minutiae, and try to control situations (4) or anxiety derived from abandonment issues.

The 5 is about movement or the lack of it. If this individual is in a situation where change is necessary and she cannot or will not make that change, her neurons (7) will receive a signal but be unable to interpret it despite numerous attempts. This can create a chaotic energy field, which overwhelms continuity and activates a seizure. This can happen in nanoseconds or over a long period.

Sexually (29/2) Transmitted (44/8) Disease (26/8) [or Diseases (27/9)] = (99/18/9) or (100/1) (STD = 7)

The 29/2 of *sexually* brings emotional tests and the possibility of emotional or physical pain and suffering into one's life if codependency is part of the equation. The 44/8 of *transmitted* reflects the opportunity for making life-altering decisions. The 26/8 of *disease* indicates a tendency to be overly involved with an other rather than taking responsibility for self-empowerment.

The numbers for *sexually transmitted disease*—a 1 (indicating low self-esteem) surrounded by three 9s—shows there is a strong need for recognition, appreciation, thanks, acceptance, and love. The three 9s can also indicate a need to control others and an inability to express love or personal feelings. The 8 indicates issues of power and control (either taking control or yielding control). Either of these patterns can cause people to not act in their highest interests (0). This may result in not saying no or practicing self-restraint.

The numbers for *sexually transmitted diseases,* 100/1, indicate feeling separate from Source (00), which results in feelings of low self-esteem (1). There is no sense of self-empowerment (8). These feelings of low self-esteem may be demonstrated by having multiple sexual partners in search of acceptance and a sense of belonging. A pattern of codependency is also present.

Finally, the initials STD transpose to the number 7—a number indicating issues of abandonment and separation. Impatience can lead people into situations they could have avoided if they'd had

140 Shingles • Sprain

```
1 2 3 4 5 6 7 8 9
A B C D E F G H I
J K L M N O P Q R
S T U V W X Y Z
```

more patience and weren't afraid of being left behind or ignored.

See also Herpes Simplex I and II *and* Human Papillomavirus Infection.

Shingles (39/12/3)

The *sh* of *shingles* equals 9, indicating a highly emotional and very intense individual who has a short fuse, wants to be loved by others (or control them), and has difficulty letting go of or expressing emotions.

The *s* on its own indicates dissatisfaction with some situation and the *h* shows an associated frustration. The *i* brings emotional intensity; the *n* an emotional roller coaster; the *g* withdrawal; the *l* emotional dissatisfaction; and *e* brings more tumultuous emotions that loop back to the original situation.

Shingles is activated by the varicella-zoster virus, which, numerically, equals 95/14/5. The triggers that release the virus are emotional (9) rigidity (5), low self-esteem (1), a need for control (4), and difficulty accepting change (5). The 14, a karmic number, indicates going to excess, whether it's being overly rigid or overly amenable. A virus always acts as an agent for change. In this case, the change required is to release emotions voluntarily, rather than forcing them to find their own way out.

To heal and dissolve the shingles, feelings of inadequacy (3) must be overcome, communication must occur in a timely and compassionate manner (2), and individuals must learn to do what they love instead of acting in order to be loved or to maintain control within relationships (9).

Sprain (32/5)

A sprain is the physical manifestation of bent or twisted emotions that have hardened and need to be loosened so they can be released. Issues involving others (2), coupled with feelings of inadequacy (3) and not being present in the moment (3 and 5), create a situation of immobility.

The 32/5 can also indicate reckless (5) behavior and scattered energy (3) while trying to impress others (2).

Adding and subtracting *spr* and *a* gives a combination of 9/7, which can indicate that at the moment of the sprain the individual was not mentally present; the mind was elsewhere.

Stress (19/1)

The 19 is a karmic number that usually brings some form of emotional distress into one's life. If everything is going well, the stress could be generated by concerns that things have been too good for too long and that they are about to change for the worse. If things are not going well, then strong emotions can make it difficult to interact with others.

Stress can be the result of putting everyone or everything else (9) ahead of the self (1) and resenting this or choosing to be emotionally isolated (1) from others by becoming a *controller* (9).

Adding and subtracting the *str* (3) and *e* (5) creates an 8/2 combination indicating that these individuals have an attitude that others should be able to read their mind or intuitively know what they want. The letter *s* appearing three times in *stress* indicates dissatisfaction with a particular state of affairs and either choosing not to do anything about it or being unable to.

Stroke (25/7)

A stroke is the result of mental (7) rigidity (5) associated with over-sensitivity (2) concerning the outcome of social interactions (2). These individuals need to be in control of almost every situation because if they're not and something goes "wrong," they feel they'll be blamed (7). Eventually, the energy expended trying to control the environment overloads the electrical circuits of the brain and "fuses" blow, shutting down specific body functions.

Stuttering (45/9)

Stuttering indicates uncertainty about expressing feelings (9), related to anxieties over rejection, abandonment, or punishment. There is an internal conflict: The 5 wants movement—it wants to do and say what it wants, whenever it wants—while the 4 is more cautious and seeks security. The negative 9 represents the two basic human behavior patterns: codependency and control, which trigger a response of wanting to speak but having anxiety over the possible consequences. When the emotions and feelings (9) of these individuals are converted into words, the flow of sound becomes erratic because of the confused signals of the simultaneous desire for independence and need to be accepted.

■ **Stutterer (38/11/2):** The brain (8) knows what it wants to say but there is so much important information at the threshold (11) that a bottleneck (8) occurs, resulting in little or no communication (2). If this happens repeatedly, the individual will withdraw (3) into himself.

Sunburn (28/1)

Sunburn is a demonstration of passive-aggressive tendencies (28). A person knows she is responsible for herself (1) but refuses to accept that responsibility. There are associated self-esteem issues (1) related to a perceived need to improve physical appearance.

Sunstroke (34/7)

Sunstroke is caused by a refusal (4) to listen to messages (3) from the higher self (7) because of a desire or need to be accepted by others (3).
   See also Stroke.

T

Illnesses and diseases beginning with the letter *T* involve intense
emotions related to interacting or communicating with others.

Temporomandibular (80/8) Disorder (47/2) = (127/10/1)

A negative 4 in relation to this disorder—be it called temporomandibular disorder, temporomandibular joint syndrome, or TMJ—*always* involves issues of control and/or constriction. This pattern often melds with the patterns associated with a negative 7. A negative 7 *always* involves issues of control or codependency, related to abandonment issues.

This condition indicates a pattern of becoming agitated (2) or frustrated (8) with people who don't listen (7) to or accept the advice (8) being given. For whatever reasons, this frustration is not expressed (7) and results in a tightening of the jaw muscles (9) that can make speaking/communicating (2) painful. The pain (4) is a call to look at the personal foundational issues that are causing this frustration and then resolve them.

The 8 of the 80 of *temporomandibular* reflects issues involving anger, frustration, personal power, money, status, and recognition. The 0 reflects not listening to the higher self.

A disorder (47/11/2) always involves things that are out of balance (2) from the way the perceiver perceives them. The 7 can indicate a messianic behavior pattern of needing to "save" people. When the 7 is combined with the 4's control/constriction pattern, self-righteousness evolves and is reflected in the negative 11. The 11, composed of two 1s, reflects the self's self-perception and perceptions of interactions with others. Thus, 11 allows a person to see the way things ought to be but usually results in frustration at not being able to make them that way.

The 127/10/1 combination indicates a need to give advice or do

(7) for others (2) to maintain a sense of self (1). The 10 indicates that it's about self-esteem and having others listen and accept the speaker's advice or wisdom in the belief that it's for their own highest good. (Notice the energy of the 11 floating through the previous sentence.)

■ **Temporomandibular (80/8) Joint (23/5) Syndrome (41/5) = (144/9) (also called TMJ, see next entry):** The 8 of the 80 of *temporomandibular* reflects issues involving anger, frustration, personal power, money, status, and recognition. The 0 of the 80 indicates not listening to the higher self.

The 23/5 of *joint* describes a pattern of mental, emotional, physical, or spiritual rigidity (5) associated with feelings of inadequacy or being unforgiving (3) toward others (2). In this condition, the joint is affected because it is a point of flexibility, and individuals with TMJ tend not to be very flexible.

A syndrome (41/5) always involves issues of self-esteem (1); control (4); and some form of mental, emotional, physical, or spiritual rigidity (5) in relation to the world (9).

The 144/9 total indicates individuals with low self-esteem (1) who have major issues involving control (44) and abandonment. They need to make certain that everyone is okay and the only way they can be certain of that is to control the situation. This is part of an abandonment anxiety pattern.

■ **TMJ (7):** The 241 combination of *TMJ* indicates a need to control or do for others because of self-esteem issues and anxieties concerning abandonment (7). If the jaw (7) is sore, communication is difficult. Less communication means less chance of saying something in anger or giving another cause to criticize this person.

See also Myofascial Pain Dysfunction, *which is associated with temporomandibular disorders.*

Thyroid (45/9) Problems (37/1) = (82/10/1)

The thyroid gland is responsible for metabolism and growth, both of which transpose to 37/1. Problems (also 37/1) with the thyroid can be traced to behavior patterns that swing between the extremes of an overactive ego ("Me first!" 1) and an underactive ego ("You go first. I insist" 2). Both extremes are related to frustration generated by concerns over personal power, social status, recognition (8), and not being able to make things happen the way they "should" happen.

The thyroid is affected when the body's emotional state (9) is out of balance. If there are too many (5) thyroid hormones, it's called hyperthyroidism; if the production of thyroid hormones is restricted (4), it's called hypothyroidism.

Hashimoto's (46/1) Thyroiditis (66/3) = (112/4): My definition of an autoimmune disorder is a condition in which all systems (mind, body, and spirit) are in disarray due to a loss of self-confidence (1), which is the catalyst for an inability to accept or even hold on to the idea of self-empowerment. With an autoimmune disorder, there can be a loss of faith that life will ever improve (4).

Hashimoto's thyroiditis is an autoimmune disorder in which antibodies (44/8) attack the thyroid gland. Since the thyroid is responsible for regulating growth (1) and metabolism (1), this condition can be seen as an attack by the "lower" self (ego, 1) on the "higher" self. It is the result of an internal confrontation between anxiety and faith (2).

The 112/4 total reveals that the self is lacking in confidence (1) and is having difficulty moving forward in life (1) without the approval or support of others (2). This can lead to procrastination, control, or stubbornness (4). A self-defeating attitude (6) associated with unrealistic expectations of self or others can stifle personal growth and the ability to metabolize life.

See also Autoimmune Disorder.

Hyperthyroidism (95/14/5): Hyperthyroidism is the result of an excessive (14 and two 5s) production of thyroid hormones. I believe that in this condition, the "ego"—which is responsible for physically supporting the soul mentally, physically, and emotionally in the third dimension—is in a hurry to prove itself (1) so as to avoid being abandoned by others (9). Swirls of preconscious emotions (9) that prevent the individual/ego (1) from grounding and centering (4) trigger hyperthyroidism.

Hypothyroidism (87/15/6): Hypothyroidism is caused by a deficiency of thyroid hormones. The effects on the body are a slowing of metabolism and lethargy (6).

The 87/15/6 combination indicates anxieties (7) over issues involving personal power, recognition, social status, and money (8) that lead the body/ego/self (1) to "hold back" or minimize expending energy (5) while it mentally (7) processes its options. What appears as lethargy (6) is really indecisiveness, which saps energy and inhibits forward movement.

Tonsillitis (50/5)

The tonsils are masses of lymphoid tissue that surround and protect the pharynx/throat from bacterial invasions. The *t* and *o* in *tonsil* and *tonsillitis* equal 8 when added together and 4 when subtracted, indicating issues concerning self-empowerment and control.

Tonsillitis (5) is an infection (5) caused by streptococcus bacteria (83/11/2). Bacteria (32/5) are harbingers of change and are activated by clumps of negatively charged particles of energy, which generate sufficient heat to alter the body temperature of adjacent areas. The heat kills off the native life-forms and allows new life-forms to incubate (3). The master number 11, appearing in *streptococcus bacteria,* grants the ability to see the way things ought to be but not always the opportunity to make them so. This leads to feelings of inadequacy (3) and frustration (8). The resolution is for these people to make others (2) be more attentive to them. This is accomplished by developing tonsillitis, which forces others to listen more closely to what *is* being said.

The 8/2 combination that results from the first and last numbers of the 83/11/2 combination indicates that another possible underlying cause of tonsillitis is wanting or expecting everyone to know what is wanted, even if it hasn't been expressed.

Tumor (24/6)

A tumor can be any increase in the size of an organ or tissue caused by the intrusion (4) of nonrelated cells (6). The 2 is the catalyst and influences the outcome of interactions with others. If the individual is a poor communicator, there is a strong probability of frustration, which can lead to encapsulating feelings and emotions. This encapsulation can burst, causing a change in the frequency of adjoining areas. This change of frequency is the beginning of a potential cancer. (*See also under* Cancer.)

The letters *t* and *u* of *tumor* added together equal 5 and subtracted equal 1, indicating a tendency to be resistant to change (5) due to self-esteem issues (1). The *u,* being the first vowel, indicates underlying anger, frustration, or repressed emotions that need to be expressed in interactions with others.

The 24/6 total reveals a pattern of becoming overly involved in the affairs of others. Whether it's a pattern involving control or the need to be needed, a driving force of this pattern is unrealistic expectations of the self and/or others, which lead to feelings of martyrdom. The 2 of the 24 can indicate difficulties letting go of emotional baggage; not speaking up in a timely manner due to anxieties over outcomes; and being overly tactful, diplomatic, or amenable.

Tumors (25/7)

Tumors indicate a rigid attitude (5) and a tendency to hold on to things of an emotional/sentimental nature (both 2s). Tumors can also

148   Tumors

1	2	3	4	5	6	7	8	9
A	B	C	D	E	F	G	H	I
J	K	L	M	N	O	P	Q	R
S	T	U	V	W	X	Y	Z	

be associated with a need to maintain control (7) because of abandonment/separation issues (7). Individuals can have difficulty letting go (5) of anxieties/fears (7) and be hypersensitive (2) to the needs of others. They have difficulty either letting go of or expressing emotions. If emotions are not expressed, they stagnate and harden (7) within the body.

Tumors can be either benign or malignant (metastatic).

Benign (33/6) Tumor (24/6) = (57/12/3): The principal challenge associated with benign tumors is learning to let go of emotions. If this can be accomplished, then the body (5) and mind (7) are rebalanced, as are the male (1) and female (2) aspects of the individual (1), and healing is accelerated. This centering of the self also prevents the spread of the cancer.

The positive number 3 is associated with creative energy, joyfulness, happiness, optimism, and the ability to communicate feelings and manifest what is desired.

Malignant (37/10/1): Despondency, pessimism, loss of joy, feelings of inadequacy (3), a chronic state of fear or anxiety revolving around abandonment issues, and a need to maintain control (7) cause a shriveling of the self (1) due to energetic exhaustion. The diminished self needs less room in the body, creating pockets of space for other energy forms to exist and thrive.

Metastatic (30/3): Despondency, pessimism, loss of joy, feelings of inadequacy, difficulty expressing emotions (3), and a sense of aloneness (0) are constrictive patterns that are stored in energy nodules. When the negative energy patterns overwhelm the positive ones, a nodule may explode and send the emotional wastes (3) into surrounding areas.

U

Illnesses and diseases beginning with the letter *U* involve unexpressed anger or frustration and poor communication

Ulcer (23/5)

An ulcer is a shallow sore produced by the destruction of skin or mucous membrane, but what causes the ulcer is a negative behavior pattern.

Ulcers may manifest in connection with a physical injury or disease but the underlying catalyst is always a behavior pattern composed of feelings of inadequacy (3); issues involving negative interactions with others (2); and a tendency to be physically, mentally, emotionally, or spiritually out of balance (5).

Ulcers are the end result of negative feelings and emotions that have been suppressed but have managed to "escape" by *eating their way to the surface* (130/4). The number 130 represents a pattern of behavior that includes low self-esteem (1), feelings of inadequacy (3), ignoring input from the higher self (0), and a need for control (4). Furthermore, 1 + 3 + 0 + 4 equals 8, a number that represents anger, frustration, and issues of empowerment. The number 13 symbolizes endings and beginnings that lead to transformations and the 0 represents spiritual support. The negative aspects of these numbers indicate patterns of denial, procrastination, control, or getting lost in details (4) out of concern that others, including Spirit (0), will not be supportive. These thoughts again stem from low self-esteem and feelings of inadequacy.

Note the frequent occurrence of the 1, 2, 3, and 5 in the numbers for the various types of ulcers listed in this section. The number 1 always deals with issues involving self; 2 always involves others; 3 is about communication and social interaction; and 5 calls for flexibility, movement, and change.

▪ **Bleeding (40) Ulcer (23/5) = (63/9):** The catalysts for this type of ulcer are issues of control (4), feelings of inadequacy (3), perfectionist tendencies (6), and an inability to release or reveal feelings (9). Bleeding is one of the body's methods for releasing waste—whether it's mental, emotional, or physical.

▪ **Duodenal (31/4) Ulcer (23/5) = (54/9):** A duodenal (31/4) ulcer indicates feelings of inadequacy (3) and low self-esteem (1), leading to procrastination or other issues involving control (4).

The 54/9 combination reveals that this condition is most likely to manifest in individuals who do *not* like change unless they are initiating it, in which case, the change can't come fast enough. All three numbers have control issues as part of their frequency. The 5 has issues with flexibility and allowing change; the 4 with how things get done as well as who will be directing; the 9 is looking for recognition and appreciation or trying to control situations so they come out "right." All of these patterns are directly linked to abandonment issues.

See also Peptic Ulcer, *below.*

▪ **Gastric (32/5) Ulcer (23/5) = (55/10/1):** With gastric ulcers, there is a core pattern of poor communication skills, poor interactions with others, issues with change, low self-esteem, and a lack of trust that higher assistance is available. When placed in positions of responsibility, these individuals frustrate themselves and possibly others because of unrealistic expectations. This is indicated by the *g* and *a* of *gastric,* which added together equals 8 and subtracted equals 6.

Notice that both *gastric* and *ulcer* reduce to 5 through different combinations of 2 and 3. This is an unusual occurrence. Also notice that the numeric total for *gastric ulcer* is 55, a master number calling for people to seek new ways of thinking and doing. Some of the patterns represented by a negative 5 are: rigidity, impulsiveness, self-indulgence, inconsistency, promiscuity, a tendency toward physical excesses, and yielding (or resisting) too quickly due to low self-esteem. Those under the influence of the negative 2 may be shy, overly sentimental, timid, careless about "things," codependent, self-centered, and prone not to speaking up for themselves. The negative 3 is associated with being moody/emotional, scattered, introverted, and vain, as well as with exaggerating and leaving things unfinished. The negative 3 brings feelings of inferiority and inadequacy and can also lead to being sarcastic, bitter, unforgiving, and even antisocial.

When the numeric frequencies of 1, 2, 3, 5, and 0 are combined, their energy creates a pattern in which an individual develops an ulcer because he feels he knows the way things ought to be but becomes frustrated that he can't make them that way. Bacteria grow because of an imbalance of intense emotions associated with a need either to be needed or to maintain control, both directly linked to abandonment issues.

See also Peptic Ulcer, *below.*

Peptic (33/6) Ulcer (23/5) = (56/11/2): The direct cause of peptic ulcers is the destruction of the gastric or intestinal mucosal lining (101/2) by hydrochloric acid (92/11/2), an acid normally present in the digestive juices (68/14/5) of the stomach. Both duodenal ulcers (54/9) and gastric ulcers (55/1) are types of peptic ulcer.

Peptic (33) indicates feelings of inadequacy strong enough to generate martyrlike behavior. Those afflicted with this condition may, in their minds, sacrifice themselves for the benefit of others (2) and then become angry and/or frustrated over not receiving recognition for their "sacrifices." There may also be a feeling of having no control over life and frustration over the inability to "make" the situation adhere to their perception of reality.

The 56/11/2 combination indicates that this category of ulcers is initiated by feeling or knowing the way things ought to be but not being able to make them that way (11). There is also a tendency toward perfectionism (6) or a sense of hyper-responsibility (6). Because 2 is the primary number of *peptic ulcer,* there are indications of imbalance in communications and relationships with others. The 5 reinforces the lack of balance in interrelationships—there is either too much flexibility or too much rigidity.

Infection with helicobacter pylori (97/16/7) bacteria is thought to play an important role in causing both gastric and duodenal ulcers. The word *infection* reduces to a number 5 (the same as *ulcer*). When we ignore the initial inflammation associated with this condition, it begins to spread, causing pain. Pain notifies us that something is amiss with our foundation. If we ignore the warning flag and attempt to mask the pain with medication, rather than dealing with the issues that caused the inflammation, an infection develops. The infection helps to focus attention on the underlying issue. If we fail to begin making changes, a chronic situation can develop.

The numbers for *helicobacter pylori* (97/16/7) indicate a pattern of acting in order to be loved or to maintain control (9) due to abandonment issues (7). This behavior is played out in the form of a messianic need to be needed or to always be right. Individuals affected by this bacterium need others to validate their importance (16/7). The 16/7 combination appears when individuals have overextended themselves mentally, emotionally, physically, or spiritually. They are being taught to release their grip and allow things to happen instead of trying to *make* them happen.

Bacteria (32/5) are agents for change. Helicobacter pylori (16/7) gains its foothold by attaching to the behavior patterns described above, which result from an imbalance of intense emotions related to abandonment (7) issues. It's interesting to note that the helicobacter pylori bacterium is the catalyst for an infection of the stomach (102/3) and the stomach is in the physical area of the third chakra, which influences feelings of well-being and self-empowerment. The numbers associated with an infection of the stomach (102/3) indicate either timidity or arrogance (1) and a tendency to ignore messages from the higher self/

Spirit (0) caused by issues involving others (2) and fueled by feelings of inadequacy or vindictiveness (3).

Urinary (43/7) Tract (17/8) Infection (50/5) = (110/2)

Notice that in both *cystitis* and *urinary,* 3 and 4 combine for a sum of 7. These numbers reveal an underlying pattern composed of behaviors driven by feelings of inadequacy, lack of control, and fears/anxieties related to abandonment or separation.

Often, these infections can be associated with engaging in sexual activity just to please a partner. The 43/7 can indicate individuals who do not stand their ground (4) due to underlying feelings of inadequacy (3) and worries over being abandoned because they are not "good enough" (7).

The message associated with this infection is to let go of self-imposed restrictions (4); communicate personal feelings (3); and release anxieties concerning rejection, embarrassment, and abandonment (7), especially in intimate relationships (whether romantic or professional).

This infection throws people off track and forces them to look at their behavior patterns. Insight can lead to the realization that infection (5) has produced an opportunity to change (5) patterns. The 17/8 of *tract* reveals apprehension about stepping into the true self (1) because of abandonment/separation issues (7), which can lead to internalized anger or frustration (8).

In summary, the 110/2 total reveals that the catalyst for this infection is an individual doing things she doesn't really want to do for the sake of keeping or maintaining a relationship (2). She knows the way things ought to be but is fearful that trying to make them that way will make her partner protest or leave (11). The 0 of the 110 indicates that this individual is ignoring the messages she is receiving from the higher self about this relationship. There can be a strong sense of feeling obligated to do things that are uncomfortable. This individual avoids acknowledging her higher self (1), thinking she's not good enough (1) and, therefore, has been abandoned by Spirit (0). This person gives her self-empowerment to an "other" (2) for love and acceptance and the illusion of security.

See also Kidney *and* Cystitis.

V

Illnesses and diseases beginning with the letter V involve issues of control and flexibility.

Vaginal (30) Infection (50) = (80/8)

The core issues are feelings of inadequacy (3), an inability to take action (5), and a failure to feel self-empowered (8) because of ignoring messages from Spirit (0).

Those afflicted with vaginal infections must overcome feelings of inadequacy (3), which can lead to constriction of the self, or withdrawal. By stuffing (5) their personal power instead of accepting it, these individuals have created a huge imbalance in the ratio of positively to negatively charged energy particles. The increase in negatively charged particles creates a reservoir of heat. As the temperature in the vaginal region rises, it changes the balance of life-forms in the area.

The total of 80 is noteworthy. A 0 always indicates the presence of Spirit, even if the presence goes unacknowledged. The 8, a power number, indicates that these individuals are wrestling with issues involving anger, frustration, personal power, money, status, and recognition. When they decide to accept their power and spiritual assistance, there will be no limit to what they can accomplish in their chosen fields.

Vaginitis (47/11/2)

Because of the 11/2 combination, the interpretation for vaginitis is basically the same as that of urinary tract infection. However, there are some differences:

The presence of the 47 indicates that the basis of the associated behavior pattern lies with major issues of abandonment (7) and control (4 and 7). The abandonment issue leads to procrastination (4). The individual procrastinates, expressing feelings in fear of rejection (7) by significant others (2). The vaginal area is near the second chakra, which deals with sexual issues. Two is the number for partnerships and communication. With vaginitis, there is a sense that the "other" is in control of the relationship.

Itis is a suffix meaning inflammation. Inflammation numerically transposes to a 1. Ultimately, vaginitis is caused by a behavior pattern rooted in low self-esteem (1) and codependency (2). The ovaries, womb, uterus, cervix, and vagina are places where women unconsciously hide or stuff their emotions (9). Over a long period of time, these constricted or "stuffed" emotions generate tremendous amounts of heat in the area of confinement. It is this heat that kills off the "normal" cells, creating "abnormal" cells a place to take root.

See also Urinary Tract Infection.

Varicose Veins (59/14/5)

Varicose veins develop most commonly in the legs but can also occur in the esophagus, in the testes, and in the anus as hemorrhoids.

The letters *v* and *a* of *varicose* can be added together for a sum of 5 or subtracted for a total of 3. This 5/3 combination indicates a tendency to resist change and even to be a bit unpleasant toward those trying to foster change.

There are constrained emotions (9) and a pattern of behavior that is either too flexible or too rigid (5). This expansion/contraction of energy eventually leads to dilated and twisted veins. The issue of flexibility/

156 Viral Infection

1	2	3	4	5	6	7	8	9
A	B	C	D	E	F	G	H	I
J	K	L	M	N	O	P	Q	R
S	T	U	V	W	X	Y	Z	

rigidity is reinforced by the number 14, a karmic number that indicates low self-esteem (1) and a need to be in control (4).

Viral (26/8) Infection (50/5) = (76/13/4)

As the twenty-second letter of the alphabet, the letter *v* of *viral* carries the energy of the master number 22. A 22 represents the ability to build on a global scale, thus enabling a viral infection to circumvent the globe.

When the word *infection* is reduced to a single digit, the digit is 5, which is about sudden and rapid changes. The 26/8 total for *viral* can be broken down as follows: The 2 deals with letting go of emotional baggage and sentimental attachments, timely communication, a willingness to compromise (win-win), and interactions with others. The 6, first and foremost, deals with accepting personal responsibility, then points to weaknesses in the autoimmune system, difficulty with intimate relationships (both physical and emotional), unfulfilled expectations, and a dash of martyrdom. The 8 represents difficulties with personal empowerment, authority, and finances. An 8 can also indicate anger, frustration, stubbornness, and materialism. The numbers 2, 4, 6, and 8 usually represent an extrovert; however, here, in their negative interpretation, they represent introverted behaviors. All of these influences combine to create a pattern of behavior in which the individual has difficulty coping with the necessity of having to make daily life-influencing decisions. The 13 indicates a need to let go mentally, emotionally, physically, and spiritually and move on to new beginnings.

A viral infection, with its 76/13/4 number pattern, reveals unrealistic expectations (6) based on anxieties associated with abandonment (7). This pattern prevents or obstructs the requirements of the 13 to learn to let go of the past, embrace the future, and make visions into reality. Failure to do this leads to procrastination and stubbornness (4). This sends a signal to the universe that a force for change must be activated and, *voilà,* a viral infection (4) catches our attention and forces us to make a decision about foundational issues and the future.

The phrase *viral infections* (plural episodes from a singular cause) equals 77/14/5. Viral infections can lead to an epidemic (4), which attacks the very foundations of civilization. Remember, a virus is an agent for change (5). The karmic number 14 indicates a pattern of excess. Whether it revolves around excess flexibility or excess rigidity, either pattern will bring sudden and unexpected change.

Looking back again at the total for *viral,* we see that disharmony (2) among groups (6)—be they cellular structures, families, businesses, or countries—breeds frustration and/or anger (8), which is a catalyst that helps the virus reach maturity.

W

Illnesses and diseases beginning with the letter *W* involve issues associated with self-confidence, moving forward, and flexibility.

Wart (17/8)

A wart results from a push-pull pattern between anger and frustration (8) over a lack of personal power (1), acceptance, or validation (7). It is caused by the human papillomavirus, which reduces to the number 7.

Warts (18/9)

Suppressed anger and frustration (8), combined with self-esteem issues (1) and either a refusal or an inability to release emotions (9), causes these emotions to bubble to the surface, solidify, and just sit there (or reoccur) until they are *consciously released* (8).

■ **Plantar (28/1) Wart (17/8) = (45/9):** If the wart is on the right side of the body (exiting), the catalyst was a passive-aggressive (28/1) attitude or a tendency to not use personal power appropriately (i.e., be overly aggressive or overly timid). If the wart is on the left side of the body (entering),

158 Weight Problem • Weight Problem (Overweight)

1	2	3	4	5	6	7	8	9
A	B	C	D	E	F	G	H	I
J	K	L	M	N	O	P	Q	R
S	T	U	V	W	X	Y	Z	

the individual is trying to stop, prevent, or isolate incoming emotional stressors (4 and 5) (i.e., stress generated by interactions at work, or with family, friends, partners, and the world at large).

The 4 and 5 reinforce a pattern of rigidity, control, and difficulty moving forward. With 9 as the total, there's a grand pattern of doing things to be loved and appreciated or controlling everything so it comes out "right," or a combination of both. In any case, there is pain (4) associated with change (5).

Weight (36/9) Problem (36/9) = (72/9)

Notice that both *weight* and *problem* transpose to 36/9 and that the final sum of *weight problem* is 9. This means that negative 9 behavior patterns dominate. One negative 9 pattern manifests in a need to be thanked, recognized, or appreciated and the other in a need to be in control. Both patterns are linked to abandonment issues.

Weight is composed of suppressed negative emotions (9). The "problem" is anxiety over being abandoned (7) by others (2). The nature of the abandonment issue can be emotional, physical, or spiritual.

Individuals may try to soothe personal feelings of inadequacy (3) by either increasing or decreasing their intake of food (6). The negative 9 reflects an ego-oriented behavior pattern of either doing things to be loved or doing things to maintain control within relationships.

With the 72/9, the negative 2 indicates that the individual is not listening to the higher self and is caught in the fear-based webs of the ego (9). As a result, the individual chooses either to become a repository for everyone's emotions (overweight) or to not hold on to any emotions (underweight).

See also Obesity.

▪ **Overweight (60/6):** The 6 indicates a tendency to assume too much responsibility for the welfare of others, much like a mother hen caring for all the little chicks in the barnyard. Because of a fear of rejection or abandonment, weight may be added to create an "emotional buffer zone" and keep others at a distance.

* **Underweight (62/8):** These individuals are unwilling to step into their personal power (8) because of past-life memories of being insensitive (2) to the feelings of others. They don't want to harm anyone with their power, so they choose to move toward invisibility. The 6 in this instance indicates difficulty in relationships (6).

* **Weight (36/9) Reduction (46/1) = (82/1):** Weight reduction is a conscious choice to release (9) emotional weight and reclaim personal (1) power (8) by interacting with others and releasing emotional attachments (2).

West (13/4) Nile (22/4) Virus (26/8) = (61/7)

The mosquito bite is the catalyst for this disease, which combines behaviors whose patterns are linked with control issues. Individuals with West Nile virus may feel that they need to do for others but not for themselves. Or they may want others to do for them or help them but never ask.

The 13/4 indicates an inability to make transitions due to low self-esteem and feelings of inadequacy. Individuals may be skeptical, need to "warn" everyone, be reactionary, procrastinate, or get lost in the minutiae of a situation.

The 22/4 indicates sensitivity issues (be it too much or too little). Individuals can be confrontational with authority figures or want approval prior to implementing ideas or plans.

In the 61/7 total, we see in the 6 the potential for unrealistic expectations of the self and others and the tendency for individuals to be perfectionists, martyrs, or everyone's cosmic mom or dad. The 1 signifies low self-esteem, which can be displayed as arrogance or timidity, or even social withdrawal. The 7 indicates people who are impatient with everything and controlling due to concerns about being blamed for the mistakes of others or judged to be less (intelligent, competent, attractive, etc.) than they perceive themselves to be. The main concern is being expelled from the group because of not "measuring up" to the group standard. There is also a need to be needed and recognized.

Y

Illnesses and diseases beginning with the letter Y involve letting go of anxiety and making decisions.

Yeast (16/7) Infection (50/5) = (66/12/3)

A yeast infection can be caused by choosing to see only the potential and not the reality of a situation. It is likely to manifest when an individual's need to be needed is greater than the actual needs of those he or she is involved with. This is a form of codependency. Yeast infections are usually found in the genital area (the area of the second chakra). The energy here is always connected with interactions with others (2), as well as low self-esteem (1) and feelings of inadequacy and scatteredness (3).

The 16/7 is a karmic number associated with an overly analytical personality. Those under the influence of this number combination seldom listen to their inner voice because of fears associated with being alone or abandoned. These individuals feel a need to be in control so that everything works well for everyone and so that they will be thanked and appreciated and no one will point the finger of failure at them.

The word *yeast* contains the same numbers that compose the core issues that are the catalysts for this infection. Note that the numeric value for the *y* and *e*, when totaled together (7 + 5 = 12, which reduces to 3), is the same number that represents the total of yeast (7) infection (5): (12/3).

Y = 7: Indecisiveness

E = 5: Emotional imbalance

A = 1: Mental need to have things a certain way

S = 1: Dissatisfaction with the current situation

T = 2: Emotional attachments, poor communication, sensitivity issues

The 66 is the number for relationships; 1 and 2 represent male and female energy as well as self-esteem and timely communication. The total of 3 is related to emotional intimacy, feelings of adequacy, optimism, and self-acceptance.

See also Candida Infection.

Conclusion

The manifestation of an illness or disease begins the moment we choose the path of self-protection, based on fears of abandonment or of being alone. This applies to those of us who consciously distance ourselves from all relationships as well as those who choose codependent relationships.

The first emotion many of us experience as we enter this dimension is fear. Fear of not knowing why we are here. Fear that we are alone here . . . unloved, unknown, and unwanted. Fear that we are being punished for something we can't remember doing. Fear that we are not in control. If we were in control, we certainly wouldn't have chosen this: being naked and alone, having nothing. These feelings originate in what Freud calls the ego: that part of the self that believes that because it is aware of its surroundings, it is reality. The other part of the self, the soul, is that part of consciousness that remembers its connection with Spirit. It realizes that it is never alone, never unloved, never unknown, and never unwanted. The soul is aware of the connection between the whole and its parts, between Spirit and its cocreators.

If we are oblivious to the fact that Spirit is always with us, if we fail to recognize that all we have to do is see the lesson before us and joyfully accept it as a gift that will help draw us closer to our divinity, we will always be in fear. Fear results in a pattern of

Failure

Excuses

Avoidance

Repetition

Fear may present itself in a variety of situations. For example, your company is downsizing and you worry that you may be on the list. If you lose your job, how will you pay the rent? How will you maintain car payments? Will your loved ones be able to finish their education? What will your family or friends think about your competence? Will you still be loved? What did you do to deserve this? In this situation, the first thing to do is ask yourself: Did I really love this job or did I do it to be loved? Was I afraid to move on? Did I begin each day filled with joy and excitement because I knew that my work fulfilled my purpose in life, that it was a way for me to express my divinity?

Whether you are losing your job or a personal relationship, be honest with yourself: Was it unfulfilling or frustrating? Were you just going through the motions? Are you fearful that people will not pay you what you are worth or love you as much as you love them? Even if you *were* fulfilled and *did* feel you were achieving your purpose, let go. Your soul, assisted by events, is trying to communicate to the ego that it is time to begin the next act in your life movie. If you have learned the lesson of surrender, you will feel the new truth in your heart. You will experience a cosmic orgasm: every layer of every one of your energy fields will vibrate into a state of synchronicity; goose bumps will ripple across your skin from head to toe. These sensations will return each time you rediscover or hear a cosmic truth.

If you see the ending of your job or relationship as a failure on your

164 Conclusion

```
1 2 3 4 5 6 7 8 9
A B C D E F G H I
J K L M N O P Q R
S T U V W X Y Z
```

part, you are coming from fear. When you come from fear, you will always see what happens to you as someone's fault.

If you rationalize an acceptable explanation to deal with this "out-of-control" situation, enter a state of denial and refuse to be in the moment, see yourself as a victim, fail to recognize this as an opportunity for self growth, you are in fear.

If you cry out "Why is this happening to me *again*?" you have failed to acknowledge where you are, how many times you have been there before, and what lesson you are to learn. You are locked in a repetitive pattern.

To break this pattern, allow vulnerability into your life. To be vulnerable is to have faith. Faith is:

Fervently loving what you do

Accepting that your soul would never create a situation that it is not capable of handling

Inspiring others by listening to your soul and following your heart

Trusting that you are one with Spirit and are supported in all that you do

Holding out an open hand and seeing the humor of the universe

Take comfort in the fact that your soul has complete knowledge of what it needs to accomplish in each lifetime and that it knows it is not alone. It knows that it is completely supported by all that ever was, is, or will be. It knows of the transitory nature of all things. It knows the pure joy of self-love and God-love. It knows it has never been abandoned, punished, or disconnected from the source of all joy . . . its own divineness. The soul has complete faith and trusts that everything unfolds as it should.

When we make "head"-based decisions, we will intellectualize, rationalize, or justify whatever we are about to do. Head-based decisions are fear-based decisions. Fear-based decisions will not bring happiness.

They will bring frustration, disappointment, and, ultimately, illness.

If you are making head-based decisions, it is because you have not integrated your soul and ego. The ego generates feelings and emotions and gives movement to the physical body. It is the repository for the soul and assists it in completing its third-dimensional mission. The relationship between the soul and the ego is much like that of a driver (soul) and car (ego); neither can go far without the help of the other. Together, the driver and car cruise the highways of life, listening to their favorite music and sharing adventures.

More often than not, the soul tries to ignore the ego and its fear-based decisions. It feels its divineness and believes that the ego holds it back. However, the ego, feeling abandoned and ignored by the soul, sabotages the soul's desire for reconnection with creation. This attitude drives a wedge between the ego and the soul. I can best explain this with a picture. We've all seen the cartoon where a dog is enticed to chase another animal and just as it is about to catch it, the dog reaches the end of its leash and is suddenly jerked backward. This situation applies to us. We may commit ourselves to the spiritual path and pursue it with determination and single-minded focus. Everything seems to fall into place when, all of a sudden, we are jerked backward. Stunned at the sudden change, we question Spirit. We are confused, even angry; haven't we been doing everything required of us? Yes, we have. But, in the process, we have neglected an important aspect of our self—the ego. It was the ego that jerked on the chain to remind the soul that this is a partnership and that the ego will no longer be ignored.

How do we get the soul and ego to work together? Try this exercise: Find a quiet place where you will not be disturbed by others or by the sounds of electrical devices. Sit down and close your eyes. Slowly inhale through your nose for a count of five. Hold this breath for a count of five and then slowly exhale through your lips for a count of five. Repeat this three times. When you feel relaxed, visualize being inside your head. As a third party, acknowledge the presence of the ego and then recognize the presence of the soul. Speaking to both at the same time, invite them to join in a dialogue about their relationship. Mentally project them out of your head and into a space where they can sit across from each other. Now, direct them to speak with each other and reach a solution that will allow them to work as a team. Once they reach a solution, thank them for their hard work and invite both back into your mental space, where they meld into a single entity. This new self will have the courage to make decisions that will enable you to evolve to your highest potential.

When you choose fear—whether the fear is associated with finances, relationships, career, or power—you will see an increase in mental, emotional, or physical ailments. When you choose the road of faith, you will be tested daily to see if you have truly surrendered to the will of the universe. These tests can run the gamut from slow drivers making you late for a meeting to the arrival of a disease based on previous patterns of behavior.

All heart-based choices guide us to where we need to be, to do what we need to do, for as long as we need to do it. It's about surrendering, trusting, allowing, and letting go of what you love the most—whether it's a relationship, idea, job, location, home, or possession—knowing that what replaces it will be better and for your highest good.

If you need help to figure out why you are here, seek out teachers, read all of the books you need to, take every class you think will help, go on a pilgrimage and visit holy sites. The bottom line is: If something feels right in your heart, do it; if it doesn't, don't.

This is much easier said than done. To do what feels right in your heart takes a great deal of courage. More often than not, when we do what we love there is conflict with those who love us or attempt to control us. Others can only ask questions; only you have the answers. Your spiritual trainers have followed your script. They have spoken the words and acted the parts you wrote for them in your life movie. The hardest choice you will ever make is the one that will lead to healing: it is to make yourself your first priority—to do *what* you love, not *to be* loved or to maintain control.

Recommended Reading

For those eager to continue learning about numbers, I have listed some of my favorite titles, ranging from the most accessible introductory texts to very technical books for those with a solid background in numerology. Several of the books here are no longer in print, but they are available in libraries, at used bookstores, and online—and are definitely worth the search.

NUMEROLOGY FOR BEGINNERS

Adrienne, Carol. *The Numerology Kit.* New York: Plume, 1988.

Brill, Michael. "Identify Anyone's Behavior Patterns in Less Than a Minute." www.awakener.com.

Dodge, Ellin. *Numerology Has Your Number: The Compleat Guide to the Science and Art of Numbers by America's Foremost Numerologist.* New York: Fireside, 1988.

Ellis, Keith. *Number Power in Nature, Art, and Everyday Life.* New York: St. Martin's Press, 1978.

Goodman, Morris C. *Modern Numerology.* North Hollywood, Calif.: Wilshire Book Co., 1978.

Jordan, Juno. *Numerology: The Romance in Your Name.* Marina Del Ray, Calif.: DeVorss & Co., 1984.

Line, Julia. *The Numerology Workbook: Understanding and Using the Powers of Numbers.* New York: Sterling Publishing, 1997.

Roquemore, Kathleen. *It's All in Your Numbers: The Secrets of Numerology.* New York: Harper & Row, 1975.

Stein, Sandra Kovacs. *Instant Numerology: A Manual for the Beginner.* North Hollywood, Calif.: Newcastle Publishing, 2001.

INTERMEDIATE NUMEROLOGY BOOKS

Bishop, Barbara J. *Numerology: The Universal Vibrations of Numbers.* St. Paul, Minn.: Llewellyn Publications, 1998.

Brill, Michael. "Know Your Numbers, Know Your Self: Discovering the *Soulutions* to Your Life's Challenges." www.awakener.com, 1999.

Buess, Lynn. *Numerology: Nuances in Relationships.* Sedona, Ariz.: Light Technology Publications, 1991.

Bunker, Dusty. *Numerology and Your Future.* West Chester, Pa.: Whitford Press, 1997.

Campbell, Florence. *Your Days Are Numbered: A Manual of Numerology for Everybody.* Marina Del Ray, Calif.: DeVorss & Co., 1982.

Connolly, Eileen. *The Connolly Book of Numbers,* vols. 1 and 2. North Hollywood, Calif.: Newcastle Publishing, 1988.

Dodge, Ellin. *You Are Your First Name.* Bloomington, Ind.: iUniverse, 2000.

Grebner, Bernice Prill. *The Day of Your Birth.* Peoria Heights, Ill.: Grebner Books, 1998.

Hitchcock, Helyn. *Helping Yourself with Numerology.* Paramus, N.J.: Reward Books, 1988.

Javane, Faith. *Master Numbers: Cycles of Divine Order.* West Chester, Pa.: Whitford, 1997.

Johari, Harish. *Numerology: With Tantra, Ayurveda, and Astrology: A Key to Human Behavior.* Rochester, Vt.: Destiny Books, 1990.

Jordan, Juno. *Your Right Action Number.* Marina Del Ray, Calif.: DeVorss & Co., 1980.

Jordan, Juno, and Helen Houston. *Your Name, Your Number, Your Destiny.* North Hollywood, Calif.: Newcastle Publishing, 1982.

Poole, Richard Elliott. *The Numeric Personality.* New York: Doubleday, 1989.

Strayhorn, Lloyd. *Numbers and You: A Numerology Guide for Everyday Living.* New York: Ballantine Books, 1987.

Valla, Mary. *The Power of Numbers.* Marina Del Ray, Calif.: DeVorss & Co., 1985.

Vaughan, Richard B. *Numbers as Symbols of Self-Discovery: Exploring Character and Destiny with Numerology.* Sebastopol, Calif.: CRCS Publications, 1986.

Zolar. *Zolar's Book of Dreams, Numbers & Lucky Days.* New York: Fireside, 1985.

ADVANCED, TECHNICAL NUMEROLOGY BOOKS

Avery, Kevin Quinn. *The Numbers of Life: The Hidden Power in Numerology.* Garden City, N.Y.: Doubleday, 1977.

Buess, Lynn. *Numerology for the New Age.* Sedona, Ariz.: Light Technology Publications, 1978.

DiPietro, Sylvia. *Live Your Life by the Numbers: Your Guide to Numerology.* New York: Signet, 1991.

Goodwin, Matthew Oliver. *Numerology: The Complete Guide,* vols. 1 and 2. North Hollywood, Calif.: Newcastle Publishing, 1981, 2000.

Javane, Faith, and Dusty Bunker. *Numerology and the Divine Triangle.* Atglen, Pa.: Schiffer Publishing, 1997.

Jeanne. *Numerology: Spiritual Light Vibrations.* Salem, Ore.: Your Center for Truth Press, 1986.

Directory of Illnesses and Diseases

BOOKS OF RELATED INTEREST

Numerology
With Tantra, Ayurveda, and Astrology
by Harish Johari

The Numerology of the I Ching
A Sourcebook of Symbols, Structures, and Traditional Wisdom
by Master Alfred Huang

A Study of Numbers
A Guide to the Constant Creation of the Universe
by R. A. Schwaller de Lubicz

Past Life Dreamwork
Healing the Soul through Understanding Karmic Patterns
by Sabine Lucas, Ph.D.

Nine Designs for Inner Peace
The Ultimate Guide to Meditating with Color, Shape, and Sound
by Sarah Tomlinson

Walking Your Blues Away
How to Heal the Mind and Create Emotional Well-Being
by Thom Hartmann

Transforming Your Dragons
How to Turn Fear Patterns into Personal Power
by José Stevens, Ph.D.

Between the Lines
Understanding Yourself and Others through Handwriting Analysis
by Reed Hayes

INNER TRADITIONS • BEAR & COMPANY
P.O. Box 388
Rochester, VT 05767
1-800-246-8648

v ANF 133.335 BRILL

Brill, M.
Or₁ Numerology for healing.

PRICE: $17.50 (9024/ANF